Dorset

40 Coast and Country Walks

The author and publisher have made every effort to ensure that the information in this publication is accurate, and accept no responsibility whatsoever for any loss, injury or inconvenience experienced by any person or persons whilst using this book.

published by
pocket mountains ltd
The Old Church, Annanside,
Moffat DG10 9HB

ISBN: 978-1-907025-648

Text and photography copyright © Patrick Kinsella 2017

A catalogue record for this book is available from the British Library

Contains Ordnance Survey data © Crown copyright and database supported by out of copyright mapping 1945-1961

Printed in Poland

Introduction

From Old Harry Rocks, Lulworth Cove and Durdle Door, all along the shore of the Jurassic Coast to Lyme Regis, via the glowing summit of Golden Cap and the one-eyed winking lighthouse at Portland Bill, Dorset is a walkers' wonderland.

The 40 walks in this guidebook range from 1.6km to 17km. The routes roam over hills and across heath, through forests and voluptuous valleys, along ridgelines and precipitous cliffs, past caves, castles, country pubs and stunning viewpoints to find vibrant villages and secret beaches.

While following them you'll come face-to-face with formative events in England's history, witness wondrous wildlife and encounter all manner of cottage industries, from community cake- and marmalade-makers to microbreweries bubbling away in back streets.

The words of Thomas Hardy hang in the air everywhere, but Dorset has fired the imagination of many writers and artists, from William Wordsworth to John Fowles (author of Lyme Regis-based *French Lieutenant's Woman*) and John Meade Falkner, who set the swashbuckling children's classic *Moonfleet* amid the historic smuggling shenanigans of Chesil Beach and Portland.

Walking through history

Dorset has been a hotbed of human activity since prehistoric times. Prior to the Romans the region was ruled by Celts, the Durotriges, who built hillforts all over the county (many of them visited in this book), especially along the border with Devon, then occupied by tribal rivals, the Dumnonii. When the Romans rocked up in 54BC, they utterly overwhelmed the locals and forever changed the face of Southern England. Many routes explained in these pages go right past Roman forts and follow ruler-straight sections of footpath that reflect roads built by the well-organised Italians.

Another wave of invaders arrived seven centuries later, with battleships and brutal berserkers. Portland suffered Britain's first Viking attack in 789AD, sending a tsunami of shock and awe across the country. Wessex's King Alfred the Great famously fronted the fightback against the Norse newcomers, becoming the first Anglo-Saxon king in the process.

The Normans – direct descendants of the Vikings – came knocking next. William the Conqueror had Corfe Castle built on a Purbeck hilltop soon after his dramatic arrival in 1066, establishing a structure that's still standing almost 1000 years later, providing a great focal point for one of this volume's inland ambles.

More story-soaked castles are found in Sherborne, where wandering Walter Raleigh based himself when he wasn't gallivanting around the New World, discovering tubers and tobacco, and harassing the Iberians.

Fear of the Spanish Armada sparked the construction of beacons and battlements along the county's Channel-facing hills in the 16th century, some of which still survive (with more added during the Napoleonic Wars), but it was an internal conflict that caused the worst carnage in post-medieval England.

Both Corfe and Sherborne's Old Castle were wrecked by Roundheads during the English Civil War, which culminated with the execution of King Charles I in 1649. Two years later, Cromwell's New Model Army pursued the murdered monarch's son (later restored as King Charles II) across the country as he fled along a route now commemorated by a long-distance walking trail, the Monarch's Way, large sections of which are touched upon here.

In 1685, Charles II's illegitimate son – James Scott, Duke of Monmouth – landed in Lyme Regis to gather support for a rebellion against his catholic uncle, King James II. He was defeated at the Battle of Sedgemoor, but his route across Dorset is remembered in the Liberty Trail, another long-distance path extensively explored within these pages.

The sleepy town of Tolpuddle was at the epicentre of a socio-political earthquake in 1833, when six farm workers were shipped to Australia for swearing an oath to protest against plunging agricultural wages. The resulting outrage influenced the birth of the trade union movement – a route in this guide follows in the Martyrs' footsteps from the scene of their 'crime' into the fields they once worked.

During WWII, Dorset's beaches were used for practice ahead of Operation Overlord, which began with D-Day on 6 June 1944. The bunkers that sheltered Churchill, Montgomery, King George VI and General Eisenhower as they watched manoeuvres are still open. Pillboxes from the same era are found beside footpaths too, along with everything from fantastic follies such as the Great Globe near Swanage to intriguing enigmas such as the Chalk Man in Cerne Abbas.

Wildlife

Dolphins are often spotted cavorting in the waves below the limestone cliffs of Durlston Head off the Isle of Purbeck, along with the occasional whale and basking shark, while Brownsea Island is famous for its populations of native red squirrels and Asian sika deer, which sometimes swim across to the mainland.

More than 420 bird species grace the coast and skylines of Dorset, including kestrels, merlin, peregrine and red-footed falcons, and several species of owl. Auks (including puffins) are sometimes seen around Portland and close to Dancing Ledge.

The rare natterjack toad is found in wetlands around Hengistbury Head, and in the county's copious woodlands hares, foxes and badgers are regularly seen. Lucky riverside ramblers might spy otters.

Jurassic Coast

A signature experience of walking in Dorset is exploring the World Heritage-listed Jurassic Coast, which extends from Old Harry Rocks to the Devon border just past Lyme Regis (and, beyond, to Exmouth). Traced for its entire 154km length by the South West Coast Path, this natural wonder is a sensational stretch of shoreline featuring fossil-strewn beaches, colourful cliffs, beautiful bays, cave-lined coves, iconic rock formations and heather-tussocked headlands.

Here you can stroll through 200 million years of intense geological activity, travelling back in time to the Triassic-Jurassic extinction event, when the sun set on every schoolchild's favourite generation of dinosaurs, including T-Rex. Beachcombers can stumble across ammonites from Charmouth to Chesil, and petrified fossil forests are found around Lulworth Cove and Durdle Door.

Conditions and considerations

This eclectic selection of walks, rambles, hikes, treks and dawdles reflects the astonishing diversity of Dorset's topography, which ranges from the craggy clifftop paths of Portland and Purbeck to the bucolic bridleways across Blackmore Vale and Cranborne Chase. The terrain is pretty gentle, although care needs to be taken on certain sections of the South West Coast Path, where erosion has made some cliffs unstable. Avoid walking along beaches below such cliffs, too, and always obey signage relating to diversions.

Each route is worth exploring many times to witness the turning of the seasons and the shifting mood of the elements that sculpt this unique landscape. None demand exceptional fitness, but Dorset does boast the highest point on the South Coast and many other steep hills besides, so be prepared for some breathtaking climbs – all amply rewarded by stunning views.

The climate is typically temperate, with plenty of sun in summer, but rain is a regular visitor throughout the year. Strong winds can occur, so take care around cliffs, which are rarely fenced off, especially when walking with children. Carry adequate warm and waterproof clothing, and drinking water. Mobile phone reception is patchy in remote areas.

Various well-signposted long-distance footpaths crisscross the county – including the epic South West Coast Path and aforementioned Monarch's Way and Liberty Trail, plus the Macmillan Way, Jubilee Trail and Hardy Way.

Dogs are welcome on most paths, so long as they are under control and don't pose a threat to sheep, cattle or wildlife. Always look out for signage, however, and be aware that some areas don't allow dogs due to the fragility of the ecosystem.

Using this guide

Each route is accompanied by an estimated time allowance and a sketch map showing key features of the area, but these should not be relied upon for navigation – topographical Ordnance Survey (OS) maps are best for this purpose. Reference to the relevant 1:25,000 OS map has been included in the intro text to each walk.

The walks are primarily circuits. Where public transport to the start/finish point of a route is available, this is indicated in the intro text, alongside parking information, but be aware some regional bus services do not run particularly regularly – especially out of season.

Dorset's southeast area has a different feel to the rest of the county which is famed for its verdant vales, wild lonely heaths and woodlands and rolling emerald hills peering across the English Channel with precious little concrete to clutter the view.

Here, instead, between Hampshire's New Forest National Park and the coast of the Isle of Purbeck, a conurbation spreads along the shore and into the hinterland, from the near-conjoined towns of Poole, Bournemouth and Christchurch, whose inhabitants account for more than half of Dorset's population. But plenty of fine walking routes remain in and around this region too, along the rivers and estuaries, and around the headlands and harbours that made this area such a popular place to work, live and play in the first place.

The Stour Valley cuts right across the county, with a long-distance walking trail tracing almost all of the river's 100km length. In the southeast it winds past the historic town of Wimborne before later joining with the Avon to charge through Christchurch Harbour into the sea.

Poole Harbour is a magnet for outdoorsy types, and many trails dissect the wetland and riparian terrain that surrounds the great Poole puddle, especially in the west. Here, it extends almost as far as the walled town of Wareham, which is framed by the Rivers Piddle and Frome, and boasts an entire forest in its backyard.

History, both ancient and modern, runs through this corner of the county just as powerfully as it does elsewhere in Dorset, with evidence of the prehistoric Celtic Durotriges tribe dotted everywhere from Hengistbury Head to Badbury Rings, high above the 17th-century Kingston Lacy estate.

King Alfred the Great did some of his best Viking vanquishing work in and around Wareham, and the entire region has been shaped by everyone from Bronze Age barrow builders to Italian and Danish invaders and homegrown smugglers. Evidence of all this lies out there on the footpaths that cavort across the terrain between the area's towns and cities – you've just got to know where to look.

Poole Harbour and Southeast Dorset

Brownsea Island

Distance 5.5km **Time** 3 hours
Terrain footpaths and beach
Map OS Explorer OL15
Access charge for non-National Trust
members; the island is open from early
February (weekends only until mid-
March) until late October; ferries from
Poole Quay and Sandbanks, parking at
both (charge); buses from Swanage and
Bournemouth to Poole and Sandbanks

There are few things more satisfying than
a walk around an island – especially one
where cars are forbidden and red squirrels
abound. This is an ideal excursion into an
environment that's so far removed from
city life it's hard to believe Poole and
Bournemouth are just across the water.

Cuddled in the embrace of Poole Harbour,
the shores of beautiful Brownsea Island are
lapped by jade-hued waters that make it so
much more appealing than its moniker
suggests. Perhaps this was deliberate – to
keep the hordes away – but if so Baden

Powell put the kibosh on that by situating
the very first scout camp here in August
1907, forever enshrining the little isle as the
birthplace of a movement that claims more
than 28 million members worldwide.

The name doesn't put off the thousands
of woggle wearers who come each year to
pay homage to that first camp, nor does it
deter hundreds of wetsuit-clad water
warriors from taking part in the annual
6.5km wild swimming race around the
island each July.

Like the swim, this very family-friendly
ramble loops the island, taking in plenty of
wildlife and history en route, including the
site of Baden Powell's camp. It traces the
south and west coasts before returning
along Middle Street which, as you'd expect
on a car-free island, is a path, not a street.
Note, the island is also dog free to protect
the famous population of red squirrels.

Disembark from the distinctive yellow
ferry at the pier to the right of Branksea
Castle – originally a fort built by Henry VIII

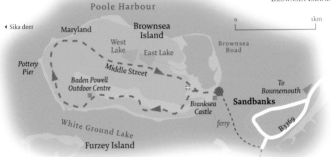

◄ Sika deer

Poole Harbour

Brownsea Island

Maryland

West Lake   East Lake

Brownsea Road

Pottery Pier

Middle Street

Baden Powell Outdoor Centre

Branksea Castle

To Bournemouth

Sandbanks

ferry

B3369

White Ground Lake

Furzey Island

0   1km

to protect Poole, now a National Trust-owned private property closed to the public.

Pass the National Trust counter and shops and continue straight on, between the castle and the Dorset Wildlife Trust-maintained wetland and lagoon. A large green space – the Church Field – soon opens up on your left, perennially populated by picnickers, peacocks and roosters, all squabbling over sandwiches.

Meander across the grass towards farm buildings, call into the visitor centre to pick up information and maps, and take the path through the trees towards the south coast. Steps lead down to a beach here, but this walk wends west through the woods, passing numerous climbing trees and viewing points peering out across the harbour to Studland and the iconic Purbeck coast, where rock formations like Old Harry are visible.

Ignore a trail forking left and continue to a T-junction. Go left, passing a turning for South Shore Lodge and then an information booth to reach a second left turn. Take this, after checking out the standing stone to the first ever scout camp, just to the right of the path.

Walk down to the shore, passing through the site of the 1907 camp, which will inevitably be occupied by a gang of modern-day scouts. Go through a gate and continue along the beach-hugging path, through the ruins of a 19th-century pottery where the shore is strewn with broken pots and parts of the path are a collage of cracked ceramics.

Pottery Pier is currently closed, so instead head inland via a set of steep steps, cross the western end of the island and explore the ghost village of Maryland. This was a thriving settlement in the 19th century, complete with a pub, but was deserted after the pottery failed and was used as a decoy during the Second World War, designed to draw bombs intended for Poole. You can access another beach here – the best spot for swimming is in the little bay just east of the spit that juts out beneath Maryland.

Return to the path, walk east until you reach the junction with Middle Street and follow this broad track all the way back to the church, keeping your eyes peeled for sika deer and, of course, the tufty-eared red squirrels that thrive on the island.

Walls and waterways of Wareham

Distance 7km **Time** 2 hours 30
Terrain historic town walls, country
footpaths and riverbank trails
Map OS Explorer OL15 **Access** buses from
Poole and Swanage; parking in Streche
Road car park, Wareham (parking charge)

**Walk the storied wonder walls of Wareham
and trace the River Piddle to the rustling
reedy shores of a nature reserve, where
hundreds of wading birds fish on the
periphery of Poole Harbour. The writhing
waterway of the Frome leads back into
town, past the historic priory, burial
ground for Dark Age kings and martyrs.**

Wareham's walls date to the time of
Alfred the Great. By 875AD, the king of
Wessex had responded to the violent
Viking invasion by setting up a system
of fortified burghs, where locals could
gather. The enormous earthy banks that
still surround the town on three sides
were among England's biggest, but that
didn't keep the Danes out in 876AD.
Fortunately, Alfred arrived, set up a
blockade and negotiated their departure,
leaving Wessex the last kingdom of Anglo-
Saxon England outside of Viking control.

This walk begins on Bloody Bank, a
section of Wareham's West Wall stained by
two macabre stories from the old town's
dark past. In 1213, a hermit called Peter de
Pomfret was tied to a horse and dragged
here from Corfe Castle, along with his son,
and then hanged for ill advisedly (and
prematurely) prophesying the end of
unpopular King John's reign. Centuries
later, after the unsuccessful Monmouth
Rebellion in 1685, infamous Judge Jeffreys
ordered five rebels to be hanged, drawn
and quartered on this spot, before
displaying their heads on spikes.

Walk onto the wall from the car park,
turn left and follow the ridge-top path
as it bends right along the banks of
the River Piddle. Continue along the

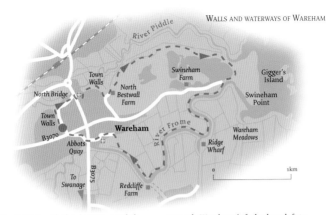

North Wall, with the river on your left, until the path dips into Shatters Hill and meets North Street, just before the bridge. Turn right here and walk about 50m until you're opposite St Martin on the Wall.

Carefully cross and skirt around this Anglo-Saxon 11th-century church, which contains a statue of Lawrence of Arabia, who was killed in a motorbike accident nearby. Go straight up St Martin's Close and left onto St Martin's Lane, then climb back onto the wall and continue around the path to a flat area used as a bowling green and archery site in Tudor times.

As the trail wends south along East Wall, look for a path leading left down to North Bestwall Road. Turn left onto this road, then follow it as it curves right and becomes a track, leading to a farm. This route segues to a footpath, part of the Poole Harbour Trail and Two Rivers Walk. Emerging from trees into fields, the River Piddle is to the far left and Bestwall Park, quarry and lake are on your right.

Follow the trail around the lake to meet the River Frome. As the path bends back

towards Wareham it forks; bear left to follow reed-fringed riverbanks past pretty boat moorings. Wareham Meadows, on your right, is home to native and migratory wading birds, including curlew, godwit and lapwing. Keep an eye to the sky too, where kestrels, peregrines, marsh harriers and sparrowhawks often hover.

The path peels away from the river and splits; ignore the right-hand option (for Bestwall Road) and go straight towards the Priory. Turn left along Conniger Lane and left again into Church Lane to wander through the grounds of the ancient minster of Lady St Mary.

Beorhtric, King of Wessex, was apparently interred here in 802AD, and this Anglo-Saxon church was the temporary burial place of King Edward the Martyr following his murder at Corfe Castle in 978AD.

Signs direct you to the close-by Quay, a lovely riverside spot for a picnic or a pint; now cross the main road and go straight up Abbots Quay. Turn right onto Tanner's Lane, then left on Pound Lane, which leads back to the car park.

Woolsbarrow Fort

Distance **3km** Time **1 hour**
Terrain **heathland and woods, footpaths
and bridleways** Map **OS Explorer OL15**
Access **parking in Stroud Bridge car park
on Sugar Hill (free)**

**Wander through the woods to explore
a little known hillfort hidden in the
heart of Wareham Forest in the southern
foothills of the Dorset Downs,
overlooking Bloxworth Heath and
the Isle of Purbeck.**

A short stroll through woodland and
heath inhabited by numerous species –
including sika deer, Dartford warblers and
even sand lizards, smooth snakes and crab
spiders – offers the perfect leg-stretcher for

those looking to break a car journey along
the A35, which scythes through the
northern end of the forest. The fact that an
ancient hillfort lies at the apex of the route
is a bonus. An enigmatic site tucked away
in the quiet corner of some conifer woods,
next to nothing is really known about
Woolsbarrow Fort, which only adds to its
attraction if you like exploring little-visited
areas of antiquity that have yet to spill their
secrets to the modern world.

Stroud Bridge car park, just north of
Wareham Forest Tourist Park, sits on the
Wareham to Bere Regis road, on a spot
where three bridleways intersect. (If the
small car park is full, another larger car
park can be found about 100m towards

Bere Regis, where a track feeds directly into the route described below.)

With your back to the road, looking ahead into the forest, take the left path leading away from the car park. Within about 300m, you will pass beneath a line of electrical pylons. Keep going straight, past a track that crosses your path (which originates from the alternative car park described above) until you reach a second junction, where the path forks. Take the right-hand option here (signed with a blue arrow), which almost immediately delivers you to the base of the hillfort.

Unlike sites such as Maiden Castle and Hambledon Hill, with their multiple halos of ditches and dykes, Woolsbarrow is a modest construction and has just one solitary rampart.

It's believed to have been built between the late Bronze Age and the early Iron Age, which makes it around 3000 years old, and it would have been populated by Dorset's Celtic tribespeople, the Durotriges. Beyond that, everything remains a mystery.

The track passes to the north of the steep-sided mound and touches the Wareham Forest Way (a 21km trail between

Wareham and Sturminster Marshall) before branching right and clambering up a curly path to a trig point at the summit, which at 67m is the highest point on the heath.

Descend, bearing left, and make sure you pick up the Wareham Forest Way, which heads directly towards the pylons (don't follow the blue arrow right in this instance, unless you parked in the alternative car park described above).

Directly below the pylons, the Forest Way soon hits a junction. The Sika Cycle Trail comes in from the left here and continues ahead, but you want to bear right, along another bridleway, back to Stroud Bridge.

◀ Heather in Wareham Forest

Highcliffe Castle to Hengistbury Head

Distance 11km **Time** 3 hours
Terrain footpaths, beach, esplanade and
ancient earthen features **Map** OS Explorer
OL22 **Access** buses from Bournemouth
and Lymington; parking in Highcliffe
Castle car park (charge in spring/summer)

From a 19th-century mansion to a
headland heaving with history and
smugglers' yarns, this shore-hugging hike
(and boat ride) across Christchurch
Harbour explores Dorset's extreme east.

*Note: Check the Mudeford ferry timetable; it's a
long walk back if you miss the last one. In
autumn/winter, the ferry runs weekends and
holidays only (mudefordferry.co.uk). The
Hengistbury loop can form a stand-alone stroll –
the headland is accessible by bus from
Bournemouth; parking (charge) by the Hiker Café.*

Built by Victorian ambassador Sir Charles
Stuart as an ostentatious family pad rather
than any sort of fort, the Gothic Revivalist
mansion known as Highcliffe Castle is an
impressive pile nevertheless. It occupies a
great spot overlooking Christchurch Bay.

If you choose to peruse the property,
you'll learn how the house historically
hosted big-name nobility, including the
Prince and Princess of Wales (later King
Edward and Queen Alexandra) and
Germany's Kaiser Wilhelm II, and was once
home to Harry Selfridge (founder of
Selfridges department store).

Wander from the house towards the sea
to enter Steamer Point Nature Reserve, a
woody clifftop sanctuary for butterflies
and birds, named after a steamboat that
was once rammed into the cliff and used as
a summerhouse. Turn right and trek
through the beach-topping treescape,
emerging below Friars Cliff to hit the hard
surface of the esplanade.

Stroll beside ever-so English beach huts
(or hurdle groynes along the sand-and-
pebble terrain of Avon Beach) to Mudeford
Quay, on the eastern arm of Christchurch
Harbour, where twin rivers, the Stour and
Avon, meet and run hand-in-hand into the
sea. Just past the Haven House Inn, a little
ferry shuttles hikers and bikers to

A337
Steamer Point
Nature Reserve
Highcliffe
Castle
Friars
Cliff
Christchurch
Avon Beach
Mudeford
0   1km
Christchurch Bay
Stanpit
Marsh
pub
Christchurch
Harbour
ferry
Double
Dykes
visitor centre
Warren Hill
Hengistbury Head

Hengistbury, a hilly headland that's been inhabited by humans since the Stone Age, when it overlooked a huge valley that was yet to flood and become the English Channel. Occupation continued throughout the ages, as evidenced by Bronze Age barrows and Iron Age fortifications still visible across the official Ancient Monument.

Wessex's Viking-vanquishing king, Alfred the Great, rebuilt the harbour in the 9th century as a defence against the invading Danes. Centuries later, intricate coves made it perfect for landing and stashing contraband, and smuggling was a huge underground industry here for decades – at one point resulting in the 1784 Battle of Mudeford, a deadly dust-up between booze-runners and customs officials.

A scattering of beach huts gives the ferry landing area a slice of shanty town-chic, and these are England's most expensive shacks. Walk to the channel-facing beach and turn right through the dunes.

Pass a pond dedicated to Britain's rarest amphibian, the noisy natterjack toad, to steps leading up East Cliff, where the anaemic Isle of Wight Needles can be seen piercing the eastern horizon.

Face west, looking along the length of the spit, and take the right-hand path, shadowing the treeline and passing ancient tumuli, to skirt around Quarry Pond, home to hundreds of birds, reptiles and insects, including dragonflies, sandmartins and swallows. Continue along South Cliff to a trig point on the headland's high point, Warren Hill, overlooking Poole Bay towards the Purbeck peninsula.

Walk west, through the heart of the nature reserve, before descending to Double Dykes, big defensive ditches dug in the Iron Age to separate the promontory from the mainland. Turn right and cross the isthmus to low-lying Barn Fields, the Hiker Café and Visitor Centre. A little land train can transport the weary-legged from here to the ferry; otherwise turn right and walk the flat harbour-hugging sealed path that goes behind the hill, keeping an eye on the freshwater lagoon for curlews, lapwings, ringed plovers, oystercatchers and shelduck.

At the quay, catch the ferry back to Mudeford and amble along the esplanade or beach to Highcliffe.

◀ The view from East Cliff

Wimborne wander

Distance 10km Time 3 hours
Terrain riverside trails, footpaths, town streets and old Roman roads
Map OS Explorer 118 Access buses from Bournemouth and Poole; parking around Wimborne Minster (parking charge)

See wonderful Wimborne Minster from every angle, while tracing the banks of the Rivers Stour and Allen as they wind around the medieval market town before converging below Canford Bridge.

The towering minster dominates Wimborne's skyline, so the best place to start this circular walk is beneath the brow of the Saxon-era church. Parts of this beautiful building are more than 1300 years old, but the Normans built most of what remains, with later generations adding a few Gothic touches. King Æthelred of Wessex (big brother of Viking-bashing Alfred the Great) was buried inside the minster in 871AD. Henry VIII half-inched most of the church's choice valuables, but it still boasts a 14th-century astronomical clock and a rare chained library, and bits of the organ date to 1664.

Walk past the Model Village and follow West Street out of town towards Julian's Bridge. Before you reach the River Stour, however, turn right into a new (and still growing) housing estate, which eventually leads to the Stour Valley Way, a footpath that chases the river across several fields.

Cross the Stour at Eye Bridge, site of an ancient weir where people have been fording the river for millennia. Follow the footpath along the predictably straight route of an old Roman road, which traverses an open meadow until the cacophonous roundabout on the A31 shatters the feeling of time travel.

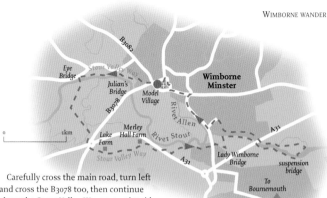

Carefully cross the main road, turn left and cross the B3078 too, then continue along the Stour Valley Way on a quiet side road running parallel to the A31, past Lake Farm and several houses.

Ducking under the A31, you emerge onto a more attractive footpath that traces the riverbank before cutting through a playground. (Avoid the temptation of turning left here to follow the river – the track simply loops around a series of private fishing spots, although you get a good eyeful of the impressive Canford Bridge overhanging the confluence of the Allen and Stour Rivers.)

Instead follow Stour Valley Way signs along streets, through an alleyway and across Oakley Hill Road, where you dogleg left towards the bridge, and then right along the riverside footpath.

About 100m in you'll encounter a fascinating feature in the elegant shape of Lady Wimborne Bridge, an amazingly ornate structure that once carried steam trains into town. Follow the 'viewpoint' sign pointing left and climb steps onto the long-redundant bridge, where a path diverges from the Stour Valley Way to head towards the river.

When the path pops out of the bushes and descends to the waterside, turn right and follow the river for around 1km, passing beneath the A31 once again, until you reach a boathouse. Cross to the opposite bank using the impressive pedestrian suspension bridge.

It's worth briefly wandering right to look back across the weir here, towards Canford Magna's 1000-year-old church and famous private school, but the route described goes left, back along the opposite riverside.

Passing under the A31 for one last time, wander along a lovely stretch of riverside path, opposite some new-build faux-Georgian houses, until the trail peels away from the waterside by a playground and boat-hire place.

At the end of the path, turn left onto Station Road and then right onto Poole Road, which traces the route of the River Allen back into town towards the minster.

◀ The River Stour

Pamphill

Distance 2.5km **Time** 1 hour
Terrain country lanes, parkland,
footpaths, bridleways and woodland
Map OS Explorer 118
Access infrequent buses from nearby
Wimborne to Pamphill; parking in
Pamphill Green car park (free)

Pamphill is a pretty little village just
outside the boundaries of Kingston Lacy
Park – the sprawling grounds which
surround a 17th-century Italian-inspired
country mansion that was once the home
of the Bankes family and is now operated
by the National Trust. However, unlike
Kingston Lacy House and Park, where
there's an entrance fee for non-members,
Pamphill's facilities are free and the area
boasts numerous nature trails and public
footpaths, which are ideal for walkers of
all abilities and ages.

From the car park off Oak Avenue, close
to St Stephen's Church to the north of
Pamphill proper, stroll south across the
grassy green. On sunny days, this idyllic
spot is typically full of families playing
games and enjoying picnics.

The village infant school, which has a
history going back more than 300 years, is
off to your left on a road that also leads to
the charismatic Vine Inn, an absolutely
tiny little pub which offers a cosy welcome
for anyone fancying a post-walk pint of
local ale.

For now, though, stay to the right of the
green, following a path that shadows the
treeline. You will meet a track at the corner
of the green, leading from the direction of
the school. Follow this right, away from
the green, and through a gate into Holly
Lane. A misleading sign here gives the
impression that this is private, but you'll

◄ Bluebells in Abbott Street Copse

soon see National Trust signage making it clear you're on the right path.

After passing a private property, a path to the left leads to a lookout point with a stunning vista over the Stour Valley, complete with a bench if you'd prefer to take in the view from a pew. This is a dead-end, however, so you'll need to retrace your footsteps and continue along the path, which itself offers good glimpses of the valley across the thatched roof of the charismatic 16th-century Holly Farmhouse that lies further down the lane towards Cowgrove.

When the path forks, keep right and cross a series of working farm fields, negotiating a number of gates and stiles. Dogs need to be kept on the lead here.

At a second fork, go right again and follow the path until it exits the fields and meets a grassy bridleway. Go right and, when you meet Sandy Lane about 100m further on, look for another distinct path leading right. This is the intriguingly named All Fools Lane – apparently an accidental corruption of the original All Souls Lane.

A few hundred metres along All Fools Lane, off to the left, you will find Abbott Street Copse, which floods with a vibrant spring tide of bluebells each May. Even outside of this annual display, which attracts lots of weekend visitors, this patch of woodland is well worth exploring for both its fauna and history – the old Roman road from Hamworthy (Poole) to Badbury Rings once ran through its midst.

After doing a loop of the copse, rejoin All Fools Lane and continue to the T-junction with Abbott Street. Turn right one more time and follow the tree-lined road to the car park.

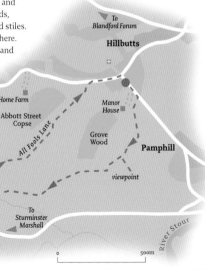

Kingston Lacy to Badbury Rings

Distance 8.5km Time 3 hours
Terrain **country lanes, tree-lined avenues,**
footpaths, bridleways, Roman roads and
the ramparts of an Iron Age hillfort
Map **OS Explorer 118** Access **infrequent**
buses from Wimborne to Kingston Lacy
Church; parking in Kingston Lacy
Gardens (note: use the free car park, not
the one at the main house)

A stroll through a diverse country
landscape and rich county history, from
the aristocratic pile of the Bankes family
to the ring-shaped remains of an Iron
Age hillfort occupied for centuries by the
ancient Celtic Durotriges people.

Myriad walking trails orbit the opulent
country mansion and gardens of Kingston
Lacy – originally home to generations of
the Bankes family after they were kicked
out of Corfe Castle for backing the wrong
side in the English Civil War.

The massive site is now owned and
managed by the National Trust, whose
members can roam the inner grounds at
will, but it's possible for everyone to freely
explore the outer area by walking the
many public footpaths that criss-cross the
bucolic landscape with its prehistoric
hillforts, Roman roads, and parks and
pastures all watered by the River Stour.

From the small car park at Kingston
Lacy Gardens – found due south of the
main house, on an elbow of Sandy Lane
just past Pamphill – walk west through
the gate and along the lane. The trees on
your right are part of a green 'belt' around
the central grounds of the main house
and park.

Ignore a left-hand turn (towards
Sturminster) and, when you reach a fork,
keep right and stick to the main lane,
which threads between Ralph and
Coneygar Copses.

◄ Beech Avenue

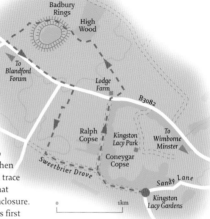

At the track's end, carefully cross busy Blandford Road and bear right around Lodge Farm, picking up a footpath that skirts the buildings and hugs a hedgerow (to your left) as it rises through fields. At the stile, cross into another field and keep climbing towards High Wood. When you reach the trees, turn left and trace the edge of the copse to a gate that opens into the Badbury Rings enclosure.

This prehistoric settlement was first inhabited up to 4000 years ago, as evidenced by Bronze Age burial mounds, and later housed a large community of Durotriges people, the Celtic tribe that lived all across Iron Age Dorset, prior to the Roman era. It's one of a series of hillforts spread across the north of the county, which includes Hambledon Hill and Hod Hill.

The site features three rings, comprised of high-standing ramparts separated by deep defensive ditches. The described trail goes anticlockwise, but you can pick any route around the ramparts, or head straight for the tree-covered centre circle, where a concrete marker details local landmarks.

When the Italian invaders arrived, they built a temple to the west of the main rings, close to where this route exits the site to follow a bridleway back to Blandford Road. There's a car park here,

near a cluster of Bronze Age burial mounds, and the lane that feeds it is part of an ancient Roman road that continues to Shapwick across the recently discovered site of the long-gone Romano-British town of Vindocladia.

Turn left along Blandford Road and try to ignore the hum of traffic as you stroll the adjacent Beech Avenue, a beautiful tunnel formed by an original planting of 731 trees by explorer and local landowner William John Bankes in 1831, which explode into colour in the autumn.

At the next junction, carefully cross Blandford Road and then turn right onto Summer Hayes Drove, which doesn't appear as a footpath on OS maps, but is waymarked as part of the National Trust's 'Route 4'. This lane meets Sweetbrier Drove, which you should follow left all the way back to Kingston Lacy Gardens.

Although set in his own era, Hardy re-invented the old Anglo-Saxon kingdom of Wessex as the geographic base for his best-known books. This semi-fictional domain was inspired, in particular, by Cranborne Chase, Blackmore Vale and the vast expanse of woods and heathland between Wareham and Dorchester.

The Dorset Hardy so deftly describes is a landscape dotted with prehistoric hillforts, interspersed with Roman remains and surviving Anglo-Saxon settlements in the shape of villages clustered around ancient abbeys, churches and castles, many built to repel the Vikings that threatened the original Wessex.

Amid all these echoes of England's past are signs of an agricultural county that struggled to cope with the Industrial Revolution, which swept across the country during Hardy's parents' lifetime. This forms the backdrop to the story of the Tolpuddle Martyrs that played out 8km from his birthplace.

The epic 350km Hardy Trail loop starts here at the author's birthplace and ends nearby where his heart lies buried. In this chapter, you can trace a more direct but no less scenic route between the same two spots, and explore all the elements of the area that inspired one of the 20th century's most influential writers.

Few areas have such a strong association with one artist as Dorset enjoys with the Victorian writer, Thomas Hardy, whose words hang in the air right across the region, but especially around Dorchester, the heathy heartland of his Wessex world.

Born and raised here, he often wandered trails as he formulated his tales, and the heaths, hills, vales and dales of Dorset form the backdrop to all his major works.

Hardy Heartland:
Central and North Dorset

Hardy's heart and soul

Distance 10km **Time** 3 hours 30
Terrain country footpaths, riverbanks, farm, heath and woodland trails
Map OS Explorer 117 or OL15
Access bus to Stinsford; parking at Hardy's Cottage, Higher Bockhampton (free)

This cradle-to-grave homage to Hardy explores terrain that influenced the author from his childhood. The route begins and ends at Hardy's birthplace, and in between strolls through Puddletown Forest and Heath, along the banks of the River Frome and into the churchyard where his heart is buried.

From the car park, take the trail leading east into the embrace of Thorncombe Wood, beneath a canopy of sweet chestnuts, oak and beech trees. Go left when the path forks, then take the next right for Hardy's Cottage.

Thomas was born here on 2 June 1840 to a stonemason father and a well-educated mother, who home schooled him until the age of eight. He returned as an adult to write *Under the Greenwood Tree* and *Far from the Madding Crowd* in the cottage.

The textures and terrain of the world immediately outside his window always influenced Hardy enormously. Themes of nature and wildlife run like footpaths through the poetry and prose he composed, and the local landscape acts like a living, breathing character in most of his work.

Following the bridleway past the cottage into Puddletown Forest is to enter the very woods and heathland that feature so prominently in Hardy's work, perhaps most notably as the somewhat sinister setting for *The Return of the Native*, in which it is renamed Egdon Heath.

Walk on, ignoring the first footpath going right. At a larger crossroads, where several tracks collide, take the sharper right turn and follow the footpath. Bhompston Heath is on your right, beyond a fence.

After about 500m you'll cross the remains of a Roman Road that stretches between Dorchester and Badbury Rings.

◄ Hardy's headstone

Duddle Heath, to your right as the path descends, boasts a series of Rainbarrows (prehistoric burial chambers).

At the bottom, pass a gate and follow a footpath through a field to the road. Carefully cross, go through Norris Mill Farm, with the buildings on your left, and take the footpath bearing right.

The path wends across functioning farmland for about 1.5km, before popping out on Bockhampton Lane at Kingston Dairy House. Turn left, carefully cross the road and go over a pretty bridge straddling the River Frome. Take the bridleway right, immediately after the bridge, and follow the beautiful banks of the river (watching out for bikes).

Ignore the first right turn and continue for about 1km, where a second right turn leads to Stinsford. The path crosses a churchyard, where you can see the Hardy family graves, including a headstone for Thomas on the spot where the writer's heart was buried after he died at the impressive age of 87 in 1928 (the rest of him was cremated and his ashes were interred in Westminster Abbey).

Exit the other side of the churchyard, walk along Church Lane

and take the second right. Follow the road around and turn right again. A footpath here leads into the grounds of Kingston Maurward College, where you can visit the gardens and animal park (and buy ice cream).

Follow the bridleway through the college complex to the Manor House, which is on your right. The bridleway then forks left, through paddocks, until it meets the road. Carefully cross, pass through a gate opposite and bear slightly right as you follow a path across two fields. When you meet the road, do a dogleg (left, then right) and walk along the lane to arrive back at the Hardy's Cottage car park.

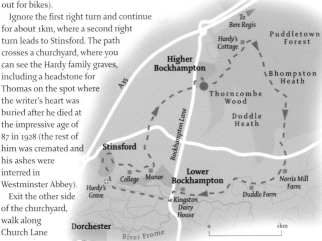

Maiden Castle

Distance 8km **Time** 2 hours
Terrain country lanes, footpaths,
bridleways, village streets and the
barrows, ditches, dykes and ramparts
of a huge prehistoric hillfort
Map OS Explorer OL15 **Access** buses from
Dorchester to Martinstown; parking
in Martinstown (free)

Maiden Castle – an immense Iron Age
hillfort where the concentric ramparts
run rings around signs of even earlier
human habitation, as well as the remains
of a Roman temple – crowns a hill high
above Dorchester. The county town
was once home to Thomas Hardy,
who features Maiden Castle in *The Mayor
of Casterbridge*.

It's perfectly possible to drive right up to
the ankles of Maiden Castle, park for free
and have a quick ramble around the
ramparts. But, when you're visiting
Europe's biggest prehistoric hillfort
– a complex structure built by the Dorset-

dwelling Durotriges people, where the
enormous Iron-Age defences encircle
evidence revealing 5500 years of human
activity – that almost seems a waste.

This is a place of such stunning physical
prominence and historic and cultural
significance that it demands to be viewed
from a distance – as the invading Romans
would have encountered it – before you
clamber around its dykes and ditches.

This route is the perfect pre-pub-lunch
perambulation, and fortunately
Winterborne St Martin (known to its
friends – and bus timetables – as
Martinstown) boasts a country inn, the
Brewers Arms, which welcomes walkers
and offers a handy car park.

The stream that gives the village its
official name, the Winterborne, flows right
beneath the pub. From the car park, walk
around the building, turn left across the
bridge and go up the lane, keeping to the
right. Take the public footpath that
branches right and follow it behind the

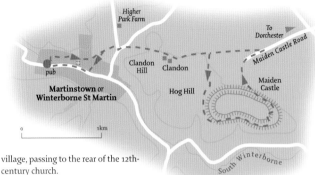

village, passing to the rear of the 12th-century church.

The path crosses a lane, leads through two gates into farm fields, then arrives at a road. Carefully cross, pick up the path (now a bridleway) opposite and continue. To your right, Clandon Hill boasts its own Bronze Age barrows.

Pass through a large farm in Clandon, looking right to get a glimpse of Maiden Castle, just beyond Hog Hill. When another bridleway intersects your path, turn right. After a gentle climb leading to a long barrow, you turn left; then, when you meet a T-junction, go straight ahead through a gate, into the site.

The ancient settlement, mostly built 800 to 300BC, is run by English Heritage. You can explore freely, often accompanied only by sheep and skylarks. Look for signs of a Neolithic causewayed enclosure that runs through the interior, from the northwest to the southeast entrances – this feature is more than 3000 years older than the rest of the structure.

This walk goes anti-clockwise around the ramparts, diverting to observe the ruined Romano-British temple and an ancient

graveyard at the eastern end. The Romans briefly occupied the site after invading Britain in 43AD, but by the end of the first century the nearby settlement of Durnovaria (modern-day Dorchester) had been founded and the hillfort was largely abandoned. The pagan temple was built a couple of centuries later.

Just beyond the temple, a gate exits the site to the right. Take this, descending some steep steps, and follow a path across the outer ditches and dykes to the main car park. Turn right along Maiden Castle Road, then take the bridleway leading left.

Pass earthworks and cross dykes on the right, before rejoining the bridleway you walked along earlier. Retrace your steps to Martinstown, crossing the road and passing through familiar fields. At the next junction, turn left along a lane and then right onto the village high street to explore the front of the Norman church and the pretty village, before arriving back at the Brewers Arms.

◀ Approaching Maiden Castle

Cerne Abbas giant thriller

Distance **4km** Time **1 hour 30**
Terrain **footpaths, bridleways, riverbank
trails, country lanes and village streets**
Map **OS Explorer 117** Access **buses from
Dorchester, Sherborne and Yeovil; parking
opposite Cerne Abbas Village Hall (free)**

**Walk on the shoulders of a great white
giant on this hill-hopping circuit across
Cerne Valley, and then explore the 1000-
year-old village that lives in the shadow
of Dorset's big nude dude.**

If Thomas Hardy's Victorian readers were
shocked by the antics of his fictional
antiheroes, imagine what they made of the
cocky Cerne Abbas Giant, prancing around
naked on a prominent hillside above a 13th-
century church and an ancient Benedictine
abbey with his weapon out (and waving a
club around too).

The mysterious multi-storey streaker –
whose 55m-tall by 51m-wide profile is

carved into the turf of Giant Hill, with the
grooves filled in with chalk – is a complete
enigma. He's been claimed as a Saxon
deity, a Celtic character and the Roman
version of the hero Hercules, but although
Cerne Abbas village predates the Norman
conquest and has been a seat of writing for
more than a millennia, the figure on the
hill above isn't mentioned until the 17th-
century, so it seems unlikely he's much
more than a sprightly 400 years old. He
may even be an epic piece of political
satire, mocking Oliver Cromwell.

It is known that some details have been
lost over time (including a cape and a
disembodied head) and others changed.
He was allegedly treated to a penis
extension at some point – when a circle
representing his naval was repurposed,
resulting in an impressive 11m erection –
and local folklore holds that proximity to
the figure helps fertility.

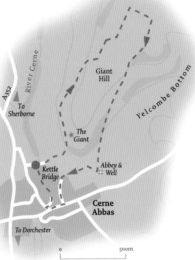

The best views of the giant are from the tables at the northern end of the picnic spot and parking area where this walk starts and finishes (or from the smaller Giant View vista spot, which drivers will pass on the way in).

From the car park, walk along Kettle Bridge Lane and cross the bridge over the River Cerne, before turning left along a footpath that curls under the cover of trees towards Giant (née Trendle) Hill. At the foot of the hill, pass through a gate and turn left along a clear path (not the trail before the gate) to ascend past the toes of the towering figure. To prevent damage to the Giant – and the Iron Age earthwork known as the Trendle (or Frying Pan) above his head, which predates him by several millennia – the National Trust, custodians of the site, have fenced them off. Keep this fence on your right while climbing the contours of the hill.

Stay right when the path forks to cross fields with views over the Cerne Valley. At a coppice, where the Wessex Ridgeway is indicated on a sign pointing left, go right again, along a bridleway across the backbone of the hill. Take another right at the next junction to follow the bridleway as it descends back towards Cerne Abbas.

At Handley's Corner the path frays four ways. Take the second right and walk towards the village, checking out the

remains of a Benedictine abbey – founded in 987AD by Æthelmær the Stout and home to St Augustine's Well, a watersource with alleged mystical properties – on the left en route. Look too for Abbot's Porch, on the right.

Shortly after passing an old burial ground, complete with preaching cross, you'll meet Abbey Street. Walk past the village pond and the 13th-century Church of St Mary the Virgin on your left to come out on Long Street, by the Royal Oak.

Turn right and pass the Giant Inn before turning right on Duck Street just after the New Inn. Take an immediate right onto Mill Lane, which leads to a peaceful path winding by the Cerne River to Kettle Bridge, beside the car park where you began.

◀ The Giant

Tolpuddle marcher

Distance 8km Time 2 hours
Terrain footpaths, bridleways, country
lanes and village streets
Map OS Explorer 117 Access buses from
Dorchester and Blandford Forum to
Tolpuddle; parking in Tolpuddle (free)

Discover the River Piddle and explore a
quiet corner of the Dorset countryside,
which in 1834 became the epicentre of a
socio-political earthquake with seismic
consequences for workers the world over.

Tolpuddle – just off the A35, 8km from
Thomas Hardy's birthplace – has a restful
rustic feel, but this seemingly
somnambulant hamlet has huge
significance in the social history of Britain.

In 1834, after enduring years of enforced
poverty while wages for rural workers were
squeezed, six Tolpuddle men – James
Brine, James Hammett, Thomas Standfield,
his son John, and brothers George and
James Loveless – formed the Friendly
Society of Agricultural Labourers.

Led by Methodist preacher George
Loveless, they swore an oath refusing to
work for less than 10 shillings a week.
Trade unions had been legal for a decade,
but the local landowner, James Frampton,
invoked an ancient law against secret
oaths and the six men were arrested, tried
(in a Dorchester court where Thomas
Hardy later worked as a magistrate),
convicted, and transported to Australia.

After 800,000 angry people signed a
petition demanding their pardon, all six
were repatriated. Their case was seminal in
the evolution of modern workers' rights
across the English-speaking world, and the
TUC organise an annual Martyrs Festival
here each July.

From the effigy outside the Tolpuddle
Martyrs Museum, march east along the
main street, turning right into the grounds
of 13th-century St John's Church. Here lies
the grave of James Hammett (the only
martyr to remain in Dorset when the
others emigrated to Canada), who died

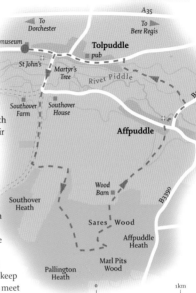

◀ Tolpuddle Martyr Memorial

in a Dorchester workhouse.

Exit the church and continue to a green triangle, where stands the Martyr's Tree – an ancient sycamore beneath which the men swore the oath – alongside a shelter dedicated to their memory. Cross the bridge over the River Piddle (a name that so embarrassed the prudish Victorians they semi-successfully changed it to Puddle, hence the variation in local place names) and walk along Southover Lane, ignoring the left turn to Southover House.

Carry straight on for 1km, then take the bridleway branching left. Ascend through fields, looking left for Piddle Valley views. Pass through a gate and keep the hedgeline on your right until you meet a copse. Turn right, and walk along a leafy bridleway through a conifer plantation.

Ignore the first two tracks leading left, but take the third, which runs between Sares Wood (left) and Pallington and Affpuddle Heaths (right). This heathland is part of the tumuli-littered landscape that Thomas Hardy used as the enigmatic Egdon Heath in *The Return of the Native* and *The Mayor of Casterbridge*.

Take the next left (and ignore subsequent right turns) to trace a serpentine bridleway slithering through the trees to Wood Barn, before crossing fields towards the scenic Saxon-era village of Affpuddle, once owned by the Frampton family, villains of the Martyr tale.

Cross the road and cut through the grounds of 13th-century St Laurence Church, turning right just before the beautiful footbridge over the Piddle to carefully exit onto the B3390.

Turn left, cross the roadbridge and cautiously walk along the pavementless B-road for 100m, before heading left into a field, where a footpath leads to a stile. Here, bear right to meet the Dorchester Road running through Tolpuddle.

Follow this left to walk through the long village, past a cottage where the Friendly Society met (marked by a TUC memorial plaque) and back to the museum, via the Martyrs Inn.

Hod Hill

Distance 3km **Time** 1 hour
Terrain country footpaths and bridleways,
open hillside, Iron Age and Roman
ramparts, and riverside trail
Map OS Explorer 118 **Access** buses from
Blandford, Sturminster Newton,
Gillingham and Yeovil to Shillingstone
and Child Okeford; parking in the NT car
park on Child Okeford Road (free)

**Ramble around Roman remains
encircled within the ramparts of an
impressive Iron Age hillfort, while
enjoying stunning views across
Cranborne Chase and rural North Dorset.
After a thigh-burning ascent at the outset,
this is an easy stroll across ancient
earthworks, followed by a lovely return
route along the banks of the River Stour.**

The car park just off the road connecting
the A350 with Child Okeford is a small

and unassuming spot, but it's a portal
through which you can go back in
time and visit Dorset as it was known
to the prehistoric Celtic tribes of the area
and the ultra-organised Romans who
subsequently steamed in and reshaped
the county.

Opposite the car park entrance is a
gate – pass through this and follow the
well-defined path that immediately sends
you hoofing up Hod Hill. Keep Hod Wood
on your near right, just the other side
of a fence, as you ascend the grassy flanks
of the hill.

After a short sharp climb up the chalky
track – ignoring a path (the Stour Valley
Way no less) that joins this route from the
left – you will pass through another gate,
with a National Trust sign confirming
you're in the right spot. This delivers you
right into the northwest corner of an

◄ Curious cow on Hod Hill ramparts

Iron Age hillfort, which itself contains the remains of a Roman camp.

The extensive earthworks that comprise Hod Hill fort were originally built around 2400 years ago, possibly as a new pad to accommodate the growing population of a long-standing Durotriges community that had been living on nearby Hambledon Hill for many generations before that.

When the Romans rocked up and ousted the locals in 43AD, they recognised both the quality of the view and the convenience of having the River Stour flowing immediately beneath the hill (the same two features that still attract legions of walkers to this spot), and promptly set up their own fort within the existing rings of ramparts and defensive ditches dug by the Durotriges.

The Stour Valley Way, which links the route described here with the Hambledon Hill walk, cuts straight across these forts, but it's more interesting to have a wander around the ramparts.

The main entrance is at the southeast corner of the fort, and that is where the Stour Valley Way exits the site, but this route continues around to the southwest corner, where a path departs the ancient defences through the deep ditches and descends the hill through the trees towards the river.

This path can be a little rough, but the route is quite clear, and when it meets the river it intersects with a well-made bank-hugging bridleway, which takes you all the way back to the car park.

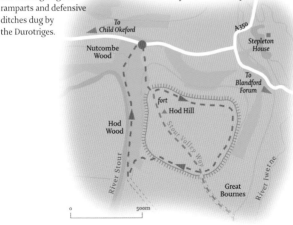

Hambledon Hill

Distance 4km **Time** 1 hour 30
Terrain country footpaths, bridleways,
open hillside and the ghost streets of a
prehistoric settlement **Map** OS Explorer
118 **Access** roadside parking in Child
Okeford (free); buses from Blandford,
Sturminster Newton, Gillingham and
Yeovil to Child Okeford

A short – but breathtakingly steep –
stroll from Child Okeford takes walkers
on a loop around the rolling ramparts of
Hambledon Hill, a naturally imposing
landmark with views across Blackmore
Vale, which was first sculpted into a fort
by the hand of man 5000 years ago and
now serves as a National Nature Reserve,
protecting numerous birds, butterflies
and wildflowers.

Starting from The Cross – a First World
War memorial opposite the Baker Arms
pub in Child Okeford – turn up Manor
Drive and enter the grounds of St Nicholas,
an attractive 16th-century stone church. Go

right around the church into the graveyard,
and exit the far gate.

Turn right onto a lane, which is soon
intersected by a public footpath, beyond
which wanderers are warned from straying
any closer to the manor house by loud
'Private' signs. Go left through the gate and
take the path across the field. Just before
you reach the road on the far side, pick up
the Stour Valley Way and follow that right,
tracing the edge of the field and looking up
at the hill that awaits your footprint.

Pass through a gate at the corner of the
field and continue along a lovely leafy
alleyway to the high heels of Hambledon
Hill. Beyond another gate, paths spider off
all over the place, but the obvious route
goes straight up, directly into the
distinctive triple-ring ramparts of one of
Britain's most impressive Iron Age hillforts.

This staggering 67-acre earthwork
complex – which contains the remains of
300 Iron Age hut platforms, a Bronze Age
burial ground and Neolithic tombs, all

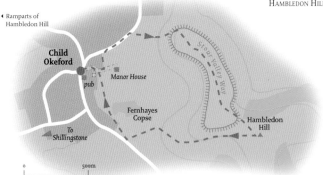

◄ Ramparts of Hambledon Hill

Child Okeford

pub

Manor House

Fernhayes Copse

To Shillingstone

Stour Valley Way

Hambledon Hill

0   500m

surrounded by deep defensive ditches, some 6km of ramparts and three main gateways – once provided a home for hundreds of members of Dorset's Celtic tribe, the Durotriges.

In August 1645, during the English Civil War, Hambledon Hill was the scene of a pitched battle between the 'Clubmen' and Oliver Cromwell's New Model Army. The Clubmen, who supported neither crown nor parliament, but were aggrieved at the destruction war was causing to their rural livelihoods, were routed by the Roundheads and the leaders were held in nearby Shroton Church, visible to the east.

Roam the route of long-extinct streets and trace the Stour Valley Way through the middle of the fort or go off-piste and ramble around the ramparts themselves, but either way follow the natural horseshoe shape of the site as it curls south, hugging the hill's natural contours.

Exiting the long barrows at the fort's southeast corner, you pass through a gate to a path running between two fences towards a concrete trig point. This is where

the earliest evidence of human habitation has been unearthed at Hambledon, and you're standing on the site of a 5000-year-old Neolithic camp.

The oldest remains discovered here – which include the body of a young man killed by an arrow – date to 2850BC, making the fort several centuries older than Egypt's Great Pyramids. It's one of a series of ancient structures that perch atop hills in this area, including neighbouring Hod Hill.

Head back towards Child Okeford by passing through the gate opposite the trig point and bearing right. While descending you'll reach the mouth of a pathway by a couple of fences, and this track leads all the way down the hill.

When you meet the road, look for a footpath shooting straight off to the right, which crosses Fernhayes Copse towards the unmistakable churchtower. When the path forks, keep right and you'll soon meet Manor Drive. Turn left and pass back through the graveyard and church grounds to pop out into the village, where the Baker Arms offers a welcome pint.

Fontmell Down

Distance 6km Time 2 hours
Terrain country lanes, public footpaths
and bridleways, Iron Age cross dykes
and wild open downland
Map OS Explorer 118 Access buses to
Fontmell Magna from Blandford,
Shaftesbury and Gillingham; parking in
Fontmell Magna (free)

The dramatic grassy fold of Fontmell
Down is a super scenic segue between
the hills of Blackmore Vale and the vast
chalk plateau of Cranborne Chase, both
areas of extraordinary natural beauty
beloved by many, including Thomas
Hardy, who invoked them as a backdrop
to several of his Wessex novels.

In memory of Hardy, the National Trust
bought 60 hectares of Fontmell Down in
1977. The site is now joint managed by the
Dorset Wildlife Trust and is home to a
kaleidoscope of flora and fauna, including
nine species of orchid, 35 different kinds of
butterfly and many mammals and birds.

Starting from the Fontmell – a pub that
literally straddles Collyer's Brook, which
flows between the bar and the dining
room – this walk goes against the flow of
Fontmell Magna's village stream, crossing
the A350 and strolling up Mill Street.
Ignore the first footpath that intersects
the road by a play area, and continue past
Springhead Cottage (on the right) to
Springhead Farm further up on the left.

A clearly-defined footpath leads left here,
ascending through a small copse to reach
the steeper flanks of Fontmell Down,
where you'll go through a gate and enter a
nature reserve, home to a spectacular
diversity of wildlife, including skylarks,
yellowhammers and stonechats.

Disregard the tracks that fork down to
the left and keep climbing into the woods.
When a bridleway crosses the path near the
summit, bear left and follow said
bridleway around the rim of the slope.
You'll soon emerge from the trees to be

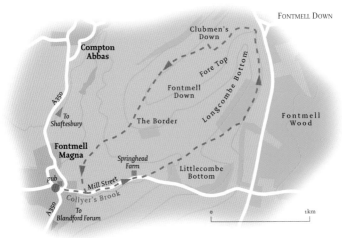

greeted with a gob-dropping view across Longcombe Bottom to the far face of Fontmell Down.

Instead of following the path as it bends right to meet the road, this walk now strays off-piste, continuing straight on to trace a contour around the curve of the precipitous chalk escarpment. Although this isn't an official footpath, there is a clear trail to follow, but don't get too distracted by small planes swooping in low to land at Compton Abbas Airfield, just off to the right.

Just after rounding the apex of this inland cove, you'll walk over an Iron Age cross dyke. Bear right here, turning your back on the lovely Longcombe Bottom vista, and pass through a gate to meet a footpath feeding in from the National Trust car park at Spread Eagle Hill.

The view now is over Compton Abbas towards Melbury Hill, and you're standing on Clubmen's Down, named after an

irregular rural fighting force that assembled here in August 1645 to do battle with Cromwell's Roundhead soldiers on nearby Hambledon Hill, in protest at the damage the Civil War was doing to their livelihoods.

Turn left and follow this path for several hundred metres along the fence, until you meet a National Trust gate. Go left through this gate, bear slightly right along a rather vague path, and descend across the open grassland of the downs to pass through another National Trust gate in the bottom corner of 'The Border'.

Keep the trees on your left and continue along the path and over a stile into another field. Cross this, go over a second stile and negotiate another field, where the path bears to the left, crosses more stiles and ultimately leads to Mill Street. Turn right and carefully follow the brook back across the main road to the pub at the starting point.

◀ Longcombe Bottom

Melbury Hill

Distance 5km **Time** 1 hour 30
Terrain country lanes, public footpaths
and bridleways, Iron Age cross dykes, wild
open downland **Map** OS Explorer 118
Access buses from Blandford, Shaftesbury
and Gillingham to nearest bus stop at
Compton Abbas; parking on Spread Eagle
Hill (free)

Melbury Hill promises panoramic views
across Dorset's dales, the colourful canvas
that Thomas Hardy superbly populated
with complex and controversial
characters, and layered with light and
shade through his nuanced narrative. As
you walk, cast your eye over the landscape
that inspired one of rural England's most
enigmatic and influential writers, and
observe clues revealing the antics of the
area's earlier inhabitants.

From the car park on Spread Eagle Hill,
head north along a footpath that runs
parallel to the busy B3081, but which is

happily separated from the ridgeline road
by trees for the most part.

After about 200m, take the path leading
left, away from the growl of engines and
across the green expanse of Compton
Down. This is a peaceful spot, but don't be
alarmed if you suddenly see a line of low-
flying light aircraft aiming straight at you –
they're preparing to land at Compton Abbas
airfield, just the other side of the road.

The path follows the fenceline to the top
of Spread Eagle Hill, then dips into a saddle
before beginning the modestly challenging
ascent of Melbury Hill. Ignore a gate and
keep the fence on your left while you climb,
looking out over the glorious immensity of
Cranborne Chase to your right.

At the summit, cross the fence to reach
the site of Melbury Beacon. Proudly
perched atop one of Dorset's highest
points, 263m above sea level, you can get
your bearings from a trig point topped
with a Diamond Jubilee memorial plate

Melbury Abbas

Melbury Hill

Melbury Beacon

◀ Melbury Hill

Compton Down

Spread Eagle Hill

Gourd's Farm

Old St Mary's Church

East Compton

0   500m

Clubmen's Down

offering directions and distances to local landmarks.

With the weather on your side, the vista from this Dorset Downs eyrie is spectacular, with Shaftesbury to the north, Cranborne Chase extending east and Blackmore Vale sprawling west – all of which feature in one guise or another in Thomas Hardy's last and most feather-ruffling Wessex novels, *Tess of the D'Urbervilles* and *Jude the Obscure*.

On clear days it's possible to glimpse Corfe Castle, the Isle of Purbeck and the English Channel to the south, providing a reminder that the original beacon once performed an important role in the defence of the country. In 1588, as the Spanish Armada threatened England's south coast, a signal beacon blazed here, part of a line of communication running between Plymouth and London.

Once you've had an eyeful of the view, head back towards Compton Down, walking on the opposite side of the fence and gazing across Compton Abbas and Fontmell Magna. After hopping over an ancient cross dyke (prehistoric ditches dug by Celtic tribes during the Iron Age), a bridleway intersects with the path. Turn right, following a track down the steep flanks of the hill.

At the bottom, the bridleway goes through a gate and skirts a farm field,

hugging a fence on the right. Walk through Gourd's Farm, turn left along the lane, and then bear right to check out the remains of old St Mary's, a tiny 15th-century church (distinct from the newer village church) that boasts a connection to an unusual chapter in the English Civil War.

In August 1645, the local reverend, Thomas Bravell, led several thousand 'Clubmen' (an armed band of locals who supported neither side in the war, but were angered by the chaos the conflict was causing) in a battle against Cromwell's New Model Army on nearby Hambledon Hill. They were defeated and, after a quick look around, you too will need to retreat to the lane you turned onto earlier.

Continue on the lane as it starts to wend left and becomes increasingly rough with warnings that it is 'Unsuitable for Motors'. Hike up this bridleway to the car park on Spread Eagle Hill at the start.

Hinton St Mary and the serpentine Stour

**Distance 5km Time 1 hour 30
Terrain village lanes, riverbank and
woodland paths Map OS Explorer 129
Access buses from Dorchester,
Gillingham, Sturminster Newton and
Yeovil; parking in Hinton St Mary (free)**

**Explore Blackmore Vale from the invisible
doorstep of a long-gone Roman Villa to a
medieval watermill on the banks of the
River Stour, then go with the flow towards
Sturminster Newton – one-time residence
of Thomas Hardy – before returning to the
warm embrace of a welcoming inn.**

The Dorset hamlet of Hinton St Mary hit
the headlines in 1963 after the extraordinary
discovery of a slab of Roman mosaic bearing
the oldest known depiction of Christ's face –
but walkers have known there's something
special about the place for decades.

The Hinton St Mary mosaic, one of the
most significant Christian-Roman finds
ever, was uncovered by chance beneath a

garden after a local man inadvertently put
a hole in it while extending the family
washing line. Dating to circa 360, when
England was a prosperous outpost of the
Italian empire, it depicts a young beardless
Jesus in Roman clobber, surrounded by
more traditional mythical imagery,
including the hero Bellerophon astride the
winged horse Pegasus, defeating the
monster Chimaera.

The original is in the British Museum,
but you can get a glimpse of the mosaic by
moseying around the village garden's
display board. This route starts nearby,
from the walker-welcoming White Horse
on Stearts Lane – where you can park if
you intend to call in for a post-wander bite
and beer.

Walk around the pub, along the length of
Old School Lane, and locate a footpath
leading to a field behind the houses. Cross
the field diagonally (bearing left) and go
right along the residential road before

◄ The White Horse

turning left on a footpath running alongside Veals Lane. When you meet Marnhull Road, carefully cross and do a slight dogleg to enter a lane opposite.

Just a few yards along this lane, the footpath leads right, through farm buildings. Emerging into the open, go diagonally across a field and pass through a gate in the hedge. Bear right, walk to the hedgeline, then turn left and head alongside the trees until a bridleway intersects the path at the end of the field.

Turn right and take this bridleway into Joyce's Coppice. Follow the trail through the trees until you emerge onto Cutt Mill Lane, where you turn left and walk towards the river and the eponymous mill.

There's been a watermill here, near the weirs, for more than 1000 years, but sadly the 18th- and 19th-century buildings that still stand were damaged by fire in 2003, and are deemed dangerous. Common sandpipers and sedge warblers still call them home, however, and it remains a peachy picnicking and paddling spot.

This is a slight diversion from the route, however, which turns left along the riverbank just before the mill and bridge. Keep the river on your immediate right as you return through Joyce's Coppice along a scenic section of the Stour Valley Way.

Keep following the flow of the river as it snakes through coppices and cow-covered fields, all the way into Sturminster Newton, which once boasted Europe's largest cattle market. About 1.5km along this path, look for a small turn to the right, which goes through a gate and across a ditch to keep you close to the river.

On the outskirts of Sturminster, the route rises away from the river, up a grassy hillside. Just before it meets the road, take the path leading left, back along the top of this meadow to enter Twinwood Coppice.

Emerging from these wonderful woods, keep the trees on your right and take the path to Wood Lane. Turn right and follow this across Marnhull Road, where it becomes Stearts Lane and leads straight back to the White Horse.

41

Sherborne castles

Distance 10km **Time** 3 hours
Terrain riverbank, forest and park paths,
town streets and a small section of road
Map OS Explorer 129 **Access** trains from
Exeter and London; buses from Yeovil and
Dorchester; parking in Sherborne (charge)

**A scenic stroll through the story-soaked
streets and country surrounds of historic
Sherborne, via an ancient abbey, through
a deer-dotted park and past two castles
eyeballing one another across a lake.**

Once the capital of the Anglo-Saxon
kingdom, Wessex, Sherborne is perhaps
best known for its link with the 16th-
century privateer, poet, soldier and queen-
whisperer, Sir Walter Raleigh, who was
leased an estate here by Elizabeth I before
falling dramatically from royal favour.

The town's two castles frame this
gallivant, but it starts by the southern wall
of Sherborne Abbey, which dates to 705AD
and contains the tombs of Alfred the
Great's two elder brothers, Wessex kings
Æthelbald and Ethelbert.

Walk down Abbey Close, turn left on Half
Moon Street, then right into Digby Road.
After about 100m, enter and walk straight
across Pageant Gardens, which historically
hosted circuses and fairs.

Exiting the gardens, go left and walk
around the train station, over a bridge
spanning the train tracks and River Yeo.
Cross the road, go through a gate into
Castle Gardens on the left, and take the
grassy path along the riverbank. On the far
side, turn left on New Road, cross back
over the river and railway line and continue
to the busy B3145.

To explore Sherborne Old Castle – a 12th-
century fortification acquired by Raleigh in
1592, ruined by parliamentary forces during
the Civil War and now owned by English
Heritage – take a diversion down Castleton
Road. Return to the B3145 and keep
walking out of town, past the Steam and
Waterwheel Centre. After around 1km, a
footpath shoots right, through a paddock,
to cut the corner with the A30. (If you miss
the stile, continue to the road junction.)

◄ Sherborne New Castle

Turn right on the noisy A30 and pound the pavement towards Oborne. After roughly 500m, look for a footpath leading right, past Old Cuthbert's Chancel, one of the last churches in England built before the Reformation. The path passes under the railway line and threads through fields and woods before meeting a junction with Pinford Lane, next to a gated entrance to the Old Castle's walled grounds.

Keep the wall on your right during a dogleg route along a path that passes directly in front of Pinford Farm. Cross a footbridge, with lake views on the right, and follow public-footpath arrows through a series of gates, over a track and up a gorgeous green hill into aptly named Deer Park, part of Sherborne Park, a medieval hunting ground that's still home to hundreds of fallow and roe deer.

After emerging from the trees and crossing a field, you'll reach a junction with a sealed track. Turn right and follow this (ignoring turnings left and right) into a thicket called the Camp. Pass buildings on your right and follow the path as it bends right and then emerges from the trees, opposite Jerusalem Hill. The path then continues straight through fields, with fantastic views over the lake and Sherborne New Castle to the right, and the Old Castle in the background.

The 'New' Castle was built by a chastened Raleigh in 1594. He had wound up in the Tower of London, along with his young wife, after unwisely upsetting Elizabeth I by impregnating and secretly marrying one of her ladies-in-waiting, Bess Throckmorton.

Once released, they retired to Sherborne Lodge (as it was called before the Old Castle was ruined) until Raleigh – an irredeemable pirate at heart – went treasure hunting around South America, in search of El Dorado and Spanish loot. When Raleigh was finally relieved of his head by James I, the estate was snapped up by the Digby family, who still own it (and charge for access, beyond the public footpaths just described).

Near Home Farm you exit the grounds through a gate. Follow the path left, descending to New Road, cross the bridge to the railway station and retrace your steps to the abbey.

Hardy Monument and Hell Stone

Distance 8km Time **2 hours**
Terrain **footpaths, farmland, bridleways
and country lanes** Map **OS Explorer OL15**
Access **buses from Poole, Weymouth,
Wareham, Bridport, Lyme Regis and
Exeter; parking in Portesham (free)**

**A trek from a hiker-friendly hostelry to
the prehistoric Hell Stone and back, via a
hilltop obelisk which celebrates the life
of one of the county's most notable sons
– a certain Thomas Hardy, but not the
one you might expect...**

Many people simply assume the Hardy
Monument – a sky-stabbing obelisk visible
from the A35 between Dorchester and
Bridport – is dedicated to Dorset's famous
writer, but it actually commemorates
another illustrious local by the same name.

Sir Thomas Masterman Hardy was flag-
captain on the *Victory* when Admiral Nelson

famously requested a kiss as his dying
wish, after being mortally wounded during
the 1805 Battle of Trafalgar. The Long
Bredy-born baronet, who subsequently
enjoyed a stellar naval career, reaching the
rank of vice-admiral, lived in Portesham
and the family owned a swathe of Black
Down, where his monument stands.

The spring-fed stream flowing through
Portesham goes right past the door of the
Kings Arms. The pub presides over a large
(often busy) car park in the village centre
and boasts a big beer garden, which makes
it the perfect start for this route.

Head through the pub's front garden
towards the phonebox, cross the road and
walk up Church Lane, behind pretty 12th-
century St Peters. Turn right onto Back
Street and round the bend to a footpath
leading left, opposite Manor Street. Follow
this path behind houses and along the

bottom of a field to a gate. Turn left along a lane, cross the farm track, go through another gate and trace the trail (now a bridleway) until you enter a copse.

Go past a pond (on your left, behind a fence marked 'private') into a large field at the foot of a hill. Ignore the temptation to walk through the gently rising middle of the meadow; instead turn right, climb the steep bank and take the footpath running along the fenceline at the top.

After about 500m, turn right through two gates onto the Inland Route/South Dorset Ridgeway (SDR). At the end of the first field, check out the stone circle, just before a gate. Walk through another field, past buildings at Hampton Barn, then cross the road to trek through more fields.

In the second field, look for a very basic stile and rather begrudging sign, indicating the location of the so-called Hell Stone - a Neolithic chambered barrow, also known as the Stone of the Dead - off to the right.

This 5000-year-old burial chamber, Dorset's only standing dolmen, was reconstructed (badly) by enthusiastic amateurs in 1866. Connected, most likely, to the nearby 'Grey Mare and Her Colts' barrow and enigmatic Valley of the Stones

on the other side of Bishop's Road, it is still well worth the brief diversion.

Return to the path, cross two more stiles to reach a wood, then turn left and ascend through Hardy Coppice to the monument celebrating the local hero, built from Portland stone on an old beacon site in 1844–5. After taking in the extraordinary views, cross the road and follow the trail descending to a small car park.

Cross the road again and pick up a path opposite (not the SDR) leading back through Benecke Wood. Pass Black Down Barn and climb briefly, before branching right along a bridleway through a gate. Keep the fence on your left until you reach an open field, then follow the wall on the right down to a lane to Portesham Hill and the village. Turn left onto Front Street and walk past Portesham House, Hardy's home until 1807, to return to the Kings Arms.

◀ Hell Stone

Not for nothing does the entire west of the county feature within the Dorset Area of Outstanding Natural Beauty. Walking routes ramble across the hilly hinterland that lies – like a lovely, albeit lumpy, green picnic blanket – behind the pebble beaches and breaking waves of Lyme Bay on the World Heritage-listed Jurassic Coast.

From verdant valley floors to Dorset's highest points, these trails wend through some of the county's most incredible countryside, taking in ancient Iron Age remains, medieval-era villages and towns, and eccentric inns and alehouses with weird and wonderful traditions (Stinging Nettle-Eating competition anyone?).

The area is studded with multiple prehistoric hillforts, because it lies on the seam between the traditional turf of two ancient peoples: the Durotriges, who settled east of the River Axe (Dorset), and the Dumnonii, who lived to the west (Devon).

Until the Romans arrived 2000 years ago and became the common foe, these rival Celtic communities vigorously defended their land and resources from one another, as evidenced by the remains of defences and fortified warrens that sit atop the upper greensand grit on the hills.

Inevitably, the Dorset bard Thomas Hardy found inspiration aplenty here, between Bridport (which is Port Bredy in *Fellow Townsmen*) and Beaminster (which is Emminster in *Tess of the d'Urbervilles*).

But Hardy wasn't the only writer to be wooed by England's wild West Country. At the end of the 18th century, William Wordsworth and his sister Dorothy spent two formative years here, regularly wandering lonely as two conjoined clouds through the hills while composing and quoting poetry out loud (a habit that convinced suspicious locals they were casting spells on their livestock).

Colmer's Hill, overlooking Chideock ▶

West Dorset

Colmer's Hill

Distance 1.6km **Time** 1 hour
Terrain footpaths, bridleways and village
lanes **Map** OS Explorer 116 **Access** buses
from Dorchester, Axminster, Exeter and
Poole to Sprakes Corner, near
Symondsbury; roadside parking in
Symondsbury (free)

Colmer's Hill erupts from the Jurassic
Coast hinterland like a great green
volcanic cone. This little loop ascends
its steep sides to quickly deliver one of
West Dorset's best vistas, with 360-degree
views far into Dorset and Devon.

Drivers on the A35 are often confronted
with the sudden sight of conical Colmer's
Hill catching the rising or setting sun on
the north of the road between Chideock
and Bridport, but few know its name or
ever stop to stagger up its steep flanks to
discover how much better the view is
from the summit.

The cheeky peak stands almost 130m
above sea level, and you will climb 107m of
that during this short, sharp hill shuffle.
The eye-popping panorama from the
summit, however, is worth every bead of
sweat invested in the ascent.

Approaching from the A35, keep left after
passing the Ilchester Arms and find a
parking spot opposite St John the Baptist
Church, amid the abundant apple orchards
of the juice- and cider-producing village
of Symondsbury.

Stroll up Shute's Lane, keeping the
church on your right, and just beyond a
bunch of houses on your left the road
segues into a rough track. After about
400m of uphill walking, a permissive path
to Colmer's Hill is signposted off to the
left. Take this and follow the path right
through the field, climbing to a huddle of
trees in a saddle between two hills.

On the other side of these trees, the path
forks, with the right-leading option
ascending to Quarry Hill. Leave that for
another day and instead go left to climb

the short, but breath-stealing path to the peak of Colmer's Hill.

This hill was once known as Sigismund's Berg after a Viking chief who barreled into Bridport with a raiding party about 1100 years ago and was impressed by the warning beacon he saw blazing on its summit (*Berg* being a Norwegian word for 'hill'). The name Symondsbury also seemingly derives from Sigismund, and this has stuck, but the hill itself was rechristened several centuries ago when it was named after a local family who were long-time tenants of the landowning Earls of Ilchester.

Planted during the First World War, seven Caledonian pines stand atop the hill, tenaciously hanging onto their turf despite the westerly winds that whip across their exposed eyrie. Beneath their bows is a trig point, by a beautiful picnic spot with 360-degree vistas. Look south to the sea and Lyme Bay is visible beyond the stunning blonde hill that is Golden Cap; to the east and north, all of West Dorset sprawls – from the Portland Peninsula to the buildings of Beaminster; while the view west is directly into the garden of Devon.

When you've had your fill of the view, descend the other side of the hill, following a clear path down the devilishly dramatic drop. Pick up too much momentum here and you won't stop until you splash into Symondsbury's supposedly sacred spring at the bottom. When someone finally gets around to launching the Hill-Rolling World Championships, this will make the ultimate venue (remember, you heard it here first, folks).

Once the terrain flattens slightly, the permissive path veers left, leading to a gate that goes past the houses and garages you passed earlier, before emerging back onto Shute's Lane. Turn right, head back into the village and check out the Ilchester Arms, a 16th-century inn armed with a big open fireplace to warm you or a cold pint of cider to cool you down, depending on the season.

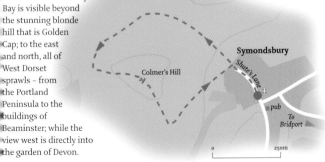

Symondsbury

Shute's Lane

Colmer's Hill

pub

To
Bridport

0   250m

Stoke Abbott and Waddon Hill

Distance **7km** Time **2 hours**
Terrain **footpaths, woodland trails and country lanes** Map **OS Explorer 116**
Access **bus from Drimpton, Bridport and Broadwindsor; parking at the New Inn, Stoke Abbott (free, walkers welcome)**

Starting and finishing at a welcoming pub with a country garden set in a medieval village at the base of a valley below a Roman fort, this stroll will get everyone stoked, from history lovers and wilderness walkers to ale-inspired amblers.

Stoke Abbott is the kind of place where traditions die hard, and the village church still performs an age-old morning wake-up call for farm workers during summer months by ringing its bell 100 times at 7am, a practice that has survived the war and complaints by blow-ins and niggly red-eyed holidaymakers (although it has moved from 5.30am since WWII).

Stoke Abbott's New Inn also rings in a traditional welcome to walkers, and the pub is the perfect starting point for this rambling route, not least because its garden makes an ideal place to enjoy a cold pint at the trail's end.

From the pub car park, cross the road and take the footpath directly opposite, passing Anchor Cottage (once the Anchor Inn) on your right. Follow the tree-lined path uphill until it emerges into fields, via a gate and stile. The path ascends the steep flanks of Waddon Hill. As you climb, pause to look back across the village of Stoke Abbott and out over the fields towards the small historic wool-industry town of Beaminster, some 10km away.

Atop Waddon Hill are the remains of a Roman hillfort, which dates to dust-ups in the mid-first century when the invading Romans, commanded by soon-to-be Roman Emperor Vespasian, were attempting to subdue Dorset's indigenous and indignant Durotriges people.

It's possible to continue through another gate and turn right to the summit, where you can explore the rough earthen banks and grassed-over features of this fort,

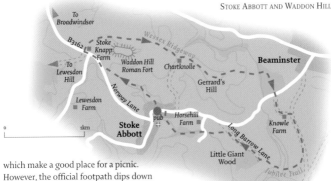

which make a good place for a picnic. However, the official footpath dips down to the left before you reach this gate (the exact route can be a little unclear, so look for signs of other walkers), then crosses a (sometimes hard-to-spot) stile before dropping steeply down a bank to meet Norway Lane.

Turn right along the lane, watching for traffic, and keep right when the road forks. Straight after the lane joins the B3162, the Wessex Ridgeway transects the road. The route left leads to Lewesdon Hill, Dorset's highest point, but this walk turns right into Stoke Knapp Farm. As you pass through the farm, a bridleway veers left, but stick to the footpath as it passes through gates and crosses fields below the dome of Waddon Hill, where the Roman ruins lie hidden.

Keep following signs for the Wessex Ridgeway as it passes a quarry to the left and doglegs through Chartknolle, where a footpath offers a cheat route back to Stoke Abbott if you want to cut the walk short. If not, carry on over Gerrard's Hill and enjoy a panoramic view across the Dorset countryside to Beaminster and beyond.

After dropping down off the hill and crossing a footbridge spanning a stream, leave the Wessex Ridgeway and turn right along a footpath that leads through fields to a road. Carefully cross, then walk up the lane opposite to Knowle Farm. Turn left through the farm, then right at the next lane. After about 500m, a stile on the right leads to a path that joins the Jubilee Trail, which takes you into the intriguingly named Little Giant Wood.

As you enter the wood, avoid crossing the first footbridge leading left and stay instead on the right bank of the stream, following the Jubilee Trail pointers to a second footbridge. Cross this, stroll through the first field and, when you enter the second one, follow the path left and then right to walk along Long Barrow Lane, which skirts a circular coppice on a hill.

About 200m further on, a path leads left towards Horsehill Farm. The track frays and splays somewhat here, and parts of it can be a little overgrown, but try to keep to the Jubilee Trail (middle option) which will deliver you back to Stoke Abbott and the New Inn.

Lewesdon Hill

Distance **8km** Time **2 hours**
Terrain **footpaths, woodland trails, lanes
and village streets** Map **OS Explorer 116**
Access **bus from Yeovil, Crewkerne and
Bridport; parking in Broadwinsor (free)**

**This ambling ascent of Dorset's highest
hill offers astonishing views across the
bucolic county – the perfect place for a
picnic as you ponder the flight of King
Charles II as he hightailed it towards
France after being turfed off the throne.**

Many Dorset villages have a Civil War tale
to tell, and Broadwinsor boasts a cracker.
After the decisive Battle of Worcester in
1651, when Oliver Cromwell's Roundheads
routed the Royalists, King Charles II legged
it through the West Country with the New
Model Army in hot pursuit. Charles was
resting overnight in Broadwinsor's village
inn when the Parliamentary troops rode

into town looking for accommodation in
the same place. Fortunately for the spaniel-
haired ex-monarch, one of the camp
followers went into labour and the
pandemonium around the birth allowed
him to escape.

A pub, The White Lion Inn, still graces
the village and after a few years of decline
it now once again offers ales and
atmosphere fit for a king. Just around the
corner the local shops have plenty of bays
for short stays of a couple of hours, which
is ample for this route (pop in and top up
on trail snacks as a courtesy).

From the shops, walk towards the White
Lion, but turn right (west) along West
Street before you reach the pub. After
about 100m, look for a footpath sign
leading left. Take this path as it leaves the
village behind, and strike out across the
fields. When the path forks, keep to the

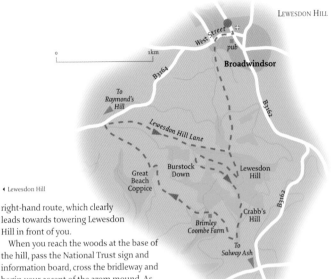

0   1km

West Street

pub

Broadwindsor

B3164

To
Raymond's
Hill

Lewesdon Hill Lane

B3162

Burstock
Down

Great
Beach
Coppice

Lewesdon
Hill

Crabb's
Hill

*Brimley
Coombe Farm*

To
Salway Ash

B3162

◄ Lewesdon Hill

right-hand route, which clearly leads towards towering Lewesdon Hill in front of you.

When you reach the woods at the base of the hill, pass the National Trust sign and information board, cross the bridleway and begin your ascent of the 279m mound. As you climb past huge oak and beech trees, keep your ears open for the rat-a-tat sound of great spotted woodpeckers and scan the forest for signs of roe deer.

At the top, where an Iron Age hillfort once stood – presumably built to take strategic advantage of the panoramic views – you have an option: carry straight on, following the main path to directly descend the south side of the hill, or turn right and walk along the precipitous edge of the escarpment, scoring more views as you stroll. This option eventually meets an old iron fence, beyond which a path drops down to join the Wessex Ridgeway (along which you will be returning later).

Before you reach this bridleway, though, look out for a little linking trail leading left to tiptoe along just beneath the route you

took across the top of the hill. After around 200m, this path meets up with the main trail that leads down from the summit (the short option mentioned above). Turn right and follow this main track, with Crabb's Hill to your left.

At the bottom, turn right and take the bridleway for a long 2km stretch, passing through Brimley Coombe Farm and doglegging across a stream at Great Beach Coppice. When the path meets the B3164, turn right along Lewesdon Hill Lane, which forms part of the Wessex Ridgeway.

Pass the junction with the path that leads up to the top of Lewesdon Hill and keep going until you meet the trail that leads back to Broadwindsor, where you can take refuge in the White Lion.

53

Wordsworth's Pen

Distance 6.5km **Time** 1 hour 30
Terrain footpaths, fields, woodland trails
and village lanes **Map** OS Explorer 116
Access buses from Yeovil, Crewkerne and
Bridport to Broadwindsor; parking in the
lay-by at the southern base of Pilsdon Pen
at the bottom of Cockpit Hill (B3164) (free)

Wander lonely as a cloud on Pilsdon Pen,
drifting around the ramparts of a pre-Iron
Age hillfort floating high above the
spectacular spread of Dorset during a
stroll that has captivated walkers and
wordsmiths for centuries.

It's hard to impress walking folk from
the Lake District, but when William
Wordsworth and his sister Dorothy came
to live in Dorset for a couple of years from
1795, the scribbling siblings soon took to
walking around Pilsdon Pen daily, so great
was their affection for the place.

For Dorothy, it provided a hint of the
hills that rise above her much-missed
Lakes, and it was in the shadow of the Pen
that 25-year-old William really began to
write in earnest (although the young
man's habit of wandering around reading
out lines of poetry apparently led to some
locals taking the indignant view that he
was putting spells on their animals).

Park in the lay-by at the beginning of
Cockpit Hill, cross the road, pass through
the gate and begin the steep ascent of the
hill that once housed a great Durotrigan
defensive and domestic structure. There's a
rest spot halfway up, but the switchbacks
take you to the top pretty quickly, where it
immediately becomes apparent why this
has been used as a vantage point by
everyone from ancient tribes to modern-
day walkers, and how useful it would have
been to those devising an early warning
system of semaphores during the
Napoleonic Wars.

At 277m, Pilsdon Pen is just a couple of
metres shy of nearby Lewesdon Hill,
making it Dorset's second tallest point, but
unlike Lewesdon, the summit is tree free.

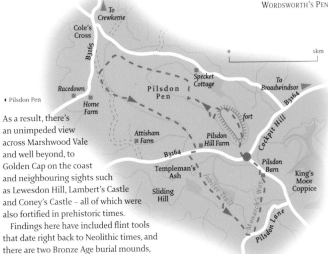

◀ Pilsdon Pen

As a result, there's an unimpeded view across Marshwood Vale and well beyond, to Golden Cap on the coast and neighbouring sights such as Lewesdon Hill, Lambert's Castle and Coney's Castle – all of which were also fortified in prehistoric times.

Findings here have included flint tools that date right back to Neolithic times, and there are two Bronze Age burial mounds, but most of the remaining features date from the Iron Age period, after which the Romans moved in and changed everything. Besides quelling the Durotriges people (through a mixture of immediate military might and gradual intermarrying), the rampaging Romans also introduced rampant rabbits to the UK, and part of the site here was a dedicated warren.

Go past the trig point and explore the multilayered defences. At the far end, pass through the final walls and look for a path leading left (west) down the hill, part of the Wessex Ridgeway. When the path forks, go right to continue along the Ridgeway.

Here, a gate is inscribed with 'Humble cares, and delicate fears' from Wordsworth's poem, 'The Sparrow's Nest', a sign that you're getting closer to the Romantic writer's old abode.

Pass a sign indicating Specket Cottage off to the right, but continue along the Ridgeway towards Cole's Cross. After passing through a couple of gates, the path veers left and drops to a T-junction, where you go left again, towards Home Farm. Here you are close to Racedown Lodge, where the Wordsworths lived for two years.

Soon after, the path splits again. Ignore Attisham Lane leading right, and carry straight on, along a bridleway. After about 1km you'll meet the B3164. Do a dogleg by turning right, crossing the road and then going left along the Jubilee Trail.

Follow this all the way down the hill, through fields, to meet Pilsdon Lane. Turn left, follow the lane briefly, and then go left again along a section of the Monarch's Way, with great views of Pilsdon Pen as you climb through fields and go via the lovely gardens of Pilsdon Barn (complete with a white unicorn) to the lay-by.

Lambert's and Coney's Castles

Distance 6km **Time** 1 hour 30
Terrain footpaths, fields, woodland trails
and village lanes **Map** OS Explorer 116
Access no buses currently serve the area;
parking at the Bottle Inn (free) or in the
National Trust car park beside Coney's
Castle (free)

From one of Dorset's most infamous pubs
– home of the annual World Nettle Eating
Championships (seriously) – this walk
loops around the ancient sites of twin
Iron Age forts, perched on hills with eye-
watering views across West Dorset and
East Devon.

The Bottle Inn in Marshwood is one of
the West Country's most notorious pubs,
not just because it is housed within a
character-drenched 16th-century thatched
building and has won multiple prizes from
CAMRA (the Campaign for Real Ale) for its
beer selection and presentation, but also
because it's the home of the World Nettle
Eating Championships.

Yep, real nettles. Being eaten. By real
people. Voluntarily and competitively.
Possibly the ultimate spectator sport. For
those rash enough to take part – or sadistic
enough to want to watch – the event
typically takes place in early June.

For everyone else, this mild meander
that links a pair of prehistoric hillforts
with commanding views across two
counties, is an all-season pleaser with no
sting in the tail.

From the Bottle Inn car park, carefully
cross the road (B3165) and set off along the
signposted footpath directly opposite the
pub, which threads between two buildings
to emerge into a field. There are two gates
on the opposite side of the field – aim for
the lower one and follow footpath signage
(which isn't featured on all gates and can
be very weathered and overgrown).

Pass Nash Farm on your left and
continue along Nash Lane, ignoring a fork
to the left, until you meet Turner's Lane.
Keep going, into Peter's Gore, where the

◀ The Bottle Inn

lanes form a quadrangle. Take the first left, and then go left again along Abbott's Wootton Lane. About 50m along this lane, a footpath branches right. Take this and follow it for around 1km as the path hugs the lower contours of a steep hill.

The path wends right to meet Long Lane. Turn right along the lane and walk up the hill. A large clearing to your left, complete with a few vague ramparts, is the site of Coney's Castle, an Iron Age hillfort which was probably used as a place to rear rabbits for food in medieval times (*coney* being the Old English word for 'rabbit').

Keep going, until you drop back down to Peter's Gore. Here, pick up the Wessex Ridgeway as it follows a good path up Lambert's Castle Hill. The eponymous 'castle' is another long-gone Iron Age hillfort, once the scene of some serious action when it was inhabited around 2500 years ago, as it lies in the old borderland between two rival Celtic tribes, the Durotriges of Dorset and the Dumnonii of Devon.

Action of a different sort took place here at least once a year between 1709 and 1947, when the plateau hosted Lambert Hill Fair, a colourful carnival of horse racing and other shenanigans. Contemplate the scene as you drink in some of the best views in the county, out over Charmouth and Chesil Beach and the restless sea to

Portland to the southeast, across Hardy country to the north, and into Devon on the west.

To descend, look for a path leading to the left (west) of the castle site, and veer right when the path forks, to meet the B3165. Turn right and then left to do a little dogleg around Turner's Lane and avoid walking along too much of the busy road, and then turn right again to stroll the last 100m back to the Bottle Inn, where you can chomp a line of nettles with a dock leaf chaser (or just have a prize-winning pint).

Stretching from the tip of **Portland** to the border with Devon, just past the popular postcard resort of Lyme Regis, the western section of Dorset's share of the Jurassic Coast is an attractive arc of fossil-strewn beaches, backed by colourful crumbly cliffs and high hilltops offering stunning views across the county.

From the famous Cobb in Lyme Regis, where the Duke of Monmouth landed in 1685 to whip up support for his ill-fated rebellion, right around to the lighthouse at Portland Bill, where beacons have been kept ablaze to warn ships of danger since Roman times and the very first Viking raids took place on British soil, this area is riddled with history and criss-crossed by beautiful walking routes.

Here, sensational sections of the South West Coast Path surf the seam between the sea and terra firma, joining the dots between fishing villages, harbour hubs, hillside hideaways, old smugglers' haunts, vanishing villages and pubs with eye-watering vistas across the waves.

This is a restless shoreline, constantly changing shape as the churning Channel takes chunks out of the coastal cliffs, and the people who maintain the paths (and those who write about them) face an endless task of repairing routes and updating details.
But it's dynamic, and the trails never get old or boring.

The hinterland has plenty of lovely long-distance trails too, many sections of which are included in walks within this chapter. These include the Monarch's Way, which sneaks along the escape route taken by King Charles II as he legged it away from his Parliamentary pursuers after losing the Battle of Worcester (the decisive dust-up in the English Civil War) in 1651, and the Liberty Trail, which follows in the footsteps of Monmouth (Charles' eldest illegitimate son) as he marched across the county to make a vain claim for the throne in 1685.

There's an abundance of natural history to be explored as well, with Charmouth Beach famous far and wide for its fossils, Chesil Beach World Heritage-listed for its uniqueness, and Portland renowned for its sturdy stone.

St Catherine's Chapel, near Abbotsbury ▶

Lyme Bay and Portland

Lyme twist

Distance 4.5km **Time** 1 hour 30
Terrain footpaths, pavement, riverbank
trails, village lanes and seafront esplanade
Map OS Explorer 116 **Access** buses from
Axminster, Bridport, Dorchester, Exeter,
Poole and Weymouth; parking at Lyme
Regis' Charmouth Road car park (charge)

**Offering a very different view of Dorset's
favourite seaside town, this walk takes a
scenic and royally rewarding approach
route, tracing parts of three long-distance
footpaths, passing through rolling fields
and following the River Lim into Lyme's
lovely backstreets. It's a secret stroll that
even many locals have never experienced.**

Lyme Regis is the jewel in Dorset's coastal
crown, a perennially popular destination
famous for everything from fish and chips
to the *French Lieutenant's Woman*, and
instantly recognisable from its distinctive
Cobb, a curvaceous breakwater that has
cuddled the historic harbour here in one
form or another since the 14th century.

It's not perfect. Parking can be a

nightmare and the front becomes
thoroughly thronged at the first hint of
blue skies. This walk circumvents these
irritations, starting from the town's
cheapest and least stressful car park to
explore little canal-lapped laneways with a
virtual Venetian feel, before emerging on
the Esplanade.

After the first few hundred metres, this
blossoms into a beautiful walk, but first
you need to come out of the car park onto
Charmouth Road, cross the street, turn
right and walk up the busy hill for about
500m, passing Timber Hill on your right
and Colway Lane on your left.

At Timber Vale Caravan Park, turn left
into the complex (there is a bridleway
fingerpost, but it's quite hidden). Walk
through the entire site, keeping left each
time the track forks, until you emerge from
the caravans onto a lane at the northwest
end of the park. Follow the path until you
meet a three-way sign pointing along
bridleways leading to Dragon's Hill, Rhode
Lane and Lyme Regis.

0   1km

◀ Lyme Regis Esplanade

Turn left (towards Lyme) and descend through fields, with Sleech Wood on your right. This path forms part of the East Devon Way and the Liberty Trail – the latter being the route followed by ill-fated farmers and rural workers who rose up in support of the Monmouth Rebellion in 1685, after the Duke of Monmouth landed at the beach near the Cobb in Lyme Regis.

At the bottom of the hill there's another intersection. This walk turns left, slightly before the badly placed sign indicating the direction of Lyme Regis. The River Lim should be on your right. The Lim was once the border between Dorset and Devon, which would have placed the Cobb in Lyme in Devon, but at some point the boundaries were shifted and all of Lyme Regis was inhaled by Dorset.

Keep following this pleasant section of the river-hugging Wessex Ridgeway/Liberty Trail as it crosses a road and enters the backstreets of Lyme, along Windsor Terrace. Here, a laneway, flanked by a canal on the left and the Lim on your right, leads into town, passing a bridge to Lepers' Well Garden, artisan shops and restaurants, a boutique brewery and the 400-year-old Guildhall, before hitting the seafront.

To check out the Cobb you need to head right, but this walk goes left around the Marine Theatre and along the Esplanade towards Charmouth and Golden Cap.

Due to landslides (historic and imminent), it's not advisable to walk the length of the beach between Lyme and Charmouth, presided over by the Spittles – part of Europe's biggest landslip. The skeletons of motor vehicles and other detritus lie rotting in the mudflows of Black Ven and high tides can trap careless wanderers against unstable and unclimbable cliffs.

However, the seawall built in 2015 provides a lovely finish to this walk, complete with fantastic views east around the Jurassic coast to Charmouth, Golden Cap and Portland. Beyond the Marine Theatre, follow this elevated Esplanade for about 300m – at low tide the rocky shoreline beside the walkway is a great place for rockpooling and crabbing. Go left at the final set of stairs, and 114 steps later you will emerge into Charmouth Road car park.

Golden Cap from Stonebarrow Lane

Distance **7km** Time **3 hours**
Terrain **footpaths, hill trails, country
lanes, clifftops and steps**
Map **OS Explorer 116** Access **parking at the
National Trust car park at Stonebarrow
(charge for non-members); buses from
Axminster, Bridport, Exeter and
Weymouth to nearby Charmouth**

**An ascent of the highest peak on Britain's
south coast, this rollercoaster ramble
richly rewards effort with far-reaching
views, a glimpse of a ghost village on the
pretty peak's western flank and a great
café at the trail's end.**

A classic – if demanding – way to climb
Golden Cap is from Charmouth, starting
along a beach liberally littered with fossils.
Currently, however, access to the peak from
the eastern end of the beach, via St Gabriel's
Mouth steps, is closed – and, despite some
maps indicating otherwise, there's no other
way to escape the pebbles until Seatown.
It's possible to be caught between the rising
tide and the unclimbable cliffs before then,
so is best avoided.

This excellent and arguably better
alternative starts 1.5km east of Charmouth.
You won't trip over any 65-million-year-old
ammonites on this amble, but conditions
underfoot are excellent. From the western
end of Stonebarrow Lane car park, pick up
the path leading southeast towards the
coast, where Golden Cap soon rears into
view. The intriguing 'Smugglers Path' forks
surreptitiously to the right, but continue
straight through Westhay Farm (look for
the wire walker sculpture). At the junction
with the South West Coast Path/Monarch's
Way), turn left.

Trace this trail as it skirts cliffs above
Charmouth Beach, meandering through
meadows often alive with butterflies. At a
stream (Westhay Water) the path dips to
cross a footbridge. Some maps indicate an
access route to the beach here, but it's long
gone and the drop-offs are dangerous.

Continue, until you reach another

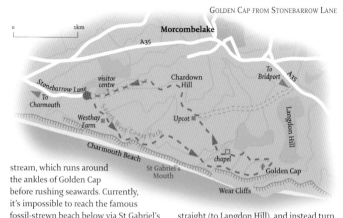

stream, which runs around the ankles of Golden Cap before rushing seawards. Currently, it's impossible to reach the famous fossil-strewn beach below via St Gabriel's Steps, because land movement and erosion around Broom Cliff have made these precipitous planks unsafe.

Instead, climb the serpentine trail scored into the side of the magnificent mound. It's a stiff, steep ascent to the 191m summit, but the views easily justify the effort. From here you can peer across Lyme Bay in both directions – to Portland on one side and Lyme Regis on the other – and look inland across the chimney tops and thatch-headed houses of umpteen villages to Hardy's literary hunting ground.

Continue over the peak of the Cap, passing a memorial stone dedicated to former National Trust chairman, the Earl of Antrim, who spearheaded Enterprise Neptune, the organisation's fight to keep coastal land open to the public. Enjoy the vista across Seatown to Thorncombe Beacon from the trig point, then start to descend via a path on the hill's northeast.

Pass through a gate, ignoring paths leading right (towards Seatown) and

straight (to Langdon Hill), and instead turn left and hug the top of the field. You'll reach another gate on your left; go through this and follow fingerposts pointing to St Gabriel's, an 800-year-old chapel that served the lost hamlet of Stanton St Gabriel until local smugglers repurposed it.

Pass through the remains of the vanished village, now just a farmhouse and some information boards, and follow signposts towards Stonebarrow. Take care to pick the right route when leaving the village, as alternative footpaths lead left to St Gabriel's Mouth and right towards Morcombelake.

This route follows a bridleway and lane before turning left, across a stile and along a footpath to dogleg through Upcot. It then arcs across Chardown Hill to arrive at Stonebarrow Lane's eastern car park, where a National Trust café serves coffee, tea, snacks and ice creams. Suitably refreshed, walk west along the lane, past an information centre housed in an old radar station, to your start point.

◀ Looking west over Charmouth Beach

Langdon Hill to Golden Cap

Distance 5km Time 1 hour 30
Terrain grassy hill trails, footpaths and
country lanes Map OS Explorer 116
Access parking at Langdon Hill National
Trust car park (charge for non-members);
bus from Weymouth, Axminster and
Bridport to nearby Chideock

The blonde-topped head of Golden Cap is
the highest point on Britain's southern
shore, and the peak is a famous feature of
the World Heritage-listed Jurassic Coast.
There are several routes to the top, but
this one, which begins on the hill's
shapely shoulders, is the easiest – and it
takes you back via one of the best pubs in
the county, with sensational sea views.

Pine- and larch-covered Langdon Hill sits
beneath the bald dome of Golden Cap like
a gorgeous green scarf draped over one
shoulder of the tallest seaside peak in the

county. The car park here, just off the A35 –
via a rather sudden turn between
Morcombelake (home of the famous
Dorset Knob biscuit since 1880) and
Chideock – is the perfect starting point for
an easy ascent of the Cap.

Leave the top end of the car park and
turn right along the very obvious track.
Follow this wide path as it orbits the hill,
clinging to a constant contourline to
eliminate any real climbing or descending
(there's plenty of that later). As you stroll,
look out for shy roe deer among the trees
and buzzards up above. If you're here in
spring or early summer, the woods will
either be awash with wild bluebells or
festooned with foxgloves.

When you reach a three-way junction at
the southern end of the hill, take the
option leading towards the coast and pass
through a gate. Directly ahead of you

is the unmistakable form of Golden Cap. Take the path leading southwest (slightly right as you face the sea) leading straight towards the sandstone summit.

Ignore a path leading left (for now) and pass through another gate to ascend the peak along a steeply climbing trail. Unsurprisingly, the view from the 191m mound is panoramic and impressive. Like an impudent ant on the head of a towering dinosaur, you're now the tallest person on the entire Jurassic Coast, which stretches 154km from Studland Bay in Dorset to Exmouth in Devon – with almost all of it visible from the peak of the Cap. Inland, it's possible to spy Pilsdon Pen and Lewesdon Hill.

When you've had your fill of views, head back down the way you came up. After passing through the first gate, however, go right and follow the footpath down the open haunch of the hill. This route, part of the South West Coast Path, descends through Black Covert and clambers around the cliffs before diving into Seatown, where the Anchor Inn awaits.

After emerging onto the road, hang a right and follow your inner divining rod to the Anchor, once the hangout of the Chideock Gang, 18th-century smugglers who allegedly used Golden Cap as a lofty lookout point. Frankly, it would be rude to pass up the chance of imbibing a pint in the spectacular beer garden here, which looks out across the curve of the coast.

When you're done, go back up Sea Hill Lane, past the footpath turning that delivered you here, and take the first lane lurching off to the left. As you walk up Pettycrate Lane, ignore the first turning to the right (Langdon Lane) and instead continue to a junction at the southern end of Langdon Hill, where you go right along a signposted footpath to complete the orbital walk you began earlier, back through the woods to the car park.

◀ Descent from Golden Cap

Thorncombe Beacon

Distance 6.5km **Time** 2 hours
Terrain grassy hill trails, clifftop paths and
country lanes **Map** OS Explorer 116
Access buses from Axminster, Bridport,
Exeter and Weymouth to nearby Chideock;
parking at Seatown (charge)

Starting and finishing at Seatown, this
classic Jurassic Coast and countryside
caper takes you along sublime sections
of two long-distance footpaths, from a
fossil-strewn beach to Eype River mouth
and back again, via an historic beacon,
prehistoric mounds and a great café.

There's parking for up to 100 cars
opposite the Anchor Inn in Seatown
(reached by turning south into Duck Street
at the church in Chideock, on the A35).
The inn sits at the top of the famously
fossil-laced shingle, right beneath Golden
Cap, the highest point on Britain's south
coast. This stroll, however, goes in the
opposite direction to a high beacon-topped
point with excellent views.

From the Anchor, head east, following
the South West Coast Path and Monarch's
Way up the hill that tops Ridge Cliff,
treading in the footsteps of the fleeing
King Charles II during his 1651 death-
defying dash to escape Parliamentary
forces after the Battle of Worcester.

Much more ancient history lies hidden
on Doghouse Hill, where National Trust
archaeologists recently unearthed evidence
of human activity dating to the Mesolithic
Age (10,000–4000BC), beside Bronze Age
pottery and the remains of a fire pit,
making this West Dorset's oldest
known settlement.

Keep the sea on your right as you edge
around cliffs above East Ebb Cove, ignoring
paths forking left, and soon you'll reach
the firebasket post that gives Thorncombe
Beacon its name. First erected in 1588 as

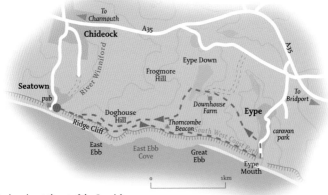

the imminent threat of the Spanish Armada caused a tsunami of fear to roll along England's south coast, this beacon was part of an early warning system and means of communication if enemy ships were spotted on the horizon.

These days it's an amazingly peaceful vantage point and picnic spot, with views stretching far and wide in both directions along the Jurassic Coast – to Golden Cap in the west and Portland to the east – and inland to the curious cone of Colmer's Hill.

Continue, following the footpath as it descends to Eype Mouth. Another good walk crosses the bridge here and continues along the coast to West Bay, but this route turns left, heading inland up Mount Lane. Pass Eype Mouth Caravan Park and then take the first left along a lane that segues into a path.

Follow this footpath uphill, passing through three gates and keeping the hedgerow on your left, until you reach Downhouse Farm, where (from March to

October) a welcoming café serves soups, light meals, cakes, coffee and cream teas.

For now, though, walk west, exiting the farm and passing through a pocket of trees before emerging into a field with Frogmore Hill on your right. Ignore the bridleway and subsequent footpath forking right to Eype Down, and instead take one of the paths leading left.

Both are good return routes to Seatown, via Doghouse Hill and Ridge Cliff, but the sharper left – which brushes the flanks of Thorncombe Beacon before turning right along a bridleway – passes between a pair of prehistoric burial mounds, purposely built (it's believed) to line up with Colmer's Hill. Known as the Devil's Jumps, because of a local legend about the Abbot of Forde Abbey booting Satan out to sea from here, there are four of these mounds in total.

Once you've bounced your own way back to Seatown, toast the coast with a brew in the Anchor Inn beer garden.

◀ Looking to Eype and Portland from Thorncombe Beacon

Eype and Bridport loop

Distance 6.5km **Time** 1 hour 30
Terrain footpaths, country lanes, clifftop
trails, pebble beach and riverside paths
Map OS Explorer 116 **Access** buses from
Dorchester, Axminster and Weymouth;
parking in Bridport A35 Rest Area (free)

**Wandering via wonderful West Bay to
beautiful Bridport by way of the South
West Coast Path, the River Brit, a brewery
and a surprising encounter with indie
rock history, this shakedown puts quiet
little Eype on the map.**

There's a café and toilets in the Bridport
Rest Area, plus free parking, making it a
practical trailhead for exploring local
villages and beaches where car space is often
at a premium. A footpath exits the back of
the rest area, cutting through trees behind
the service block to emerge by the bridge
over the busy A35. Turn right, away from the
bridge, and walk about 100m up Broad Lane,
then follow a footpath signposted left,
which shadows Mount Lane.

The path rejoins the road at a T-junction.
Cross straight over and continue along
Mount Lane towards Eype, until you pass
St Peter's, an unassuming 19th-century
church on your left with a secret second
life as an arts centre. In 2010,
internationally acclaimed West Dorset
musician P J Harvey recorded her Mercury
Prize-winning album *Let England Shake* here,
which is easily the most exciting thing that
has happened in tranquil Eype.

Just past the church, a stile leads left to a
footpath that takes you off the tarmac – a
good thing, because the lane gets very
narrow soon afterwards, with little passing
room for pedestrians and cars. Note: this
path bypasses the village pub, the New Inn
(but you've barely earned a thirst yet).

When path and lane meet again, you have
to keep to the sealed surface for a section,
but it's wider here. Carefully continue past
Eype's Mouth Country Hotel, cross the

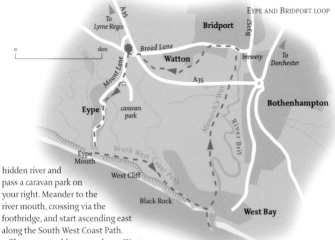

hidden river and pass a caravan park on your right. Meander to the river mouth, crossing via the footbridge, and start ascending east along the South West Coast Path.

The route rambles up and over West Cliff, a rather ashen-faced edifice compared to its counterpart on the other side of West Bay. When the sun ignites it, East Cliff (straight ahead) burns indignantly at the lack of imagination employed by whoever named the local features around here by radiating a positively golden glow and providing a fiery foreground to a fantastic view that stretches around the coast to Portland from the apex of the path.

East Cliff forms part of another walk but for a good gander at this ruddy Triassic-era tooth in the bite mark of Lyme Bay, wander along the harbour wall once you reach the scenic seaside settlement of West Bay.

From here, turn towards the town (a good place to grab lunch), cross the roundabout and, keeping the River Brit on your right, walk through the sprawling caravan park. It's not well signposted, but a footpath – the Monarch's Way – traverses this park, emerging at the northern end to cross riparian meadows (sadly, the river itself often writhes out of sight) and wriggle beneath the A35, arriving in the outskirts of Bridport, an arty market town with Saxon roots.

The path follows a pretty waterside section here, passing – near the confluence of the Rivers Brit and Asker – Palmers Brewery, which is the only thatched brewery in Britain (tours run Easter to October weekdays at 11am).

Turn left onto Skilling Hill Road to pass playing fields on your left and, when the pavement runs out, continue (carefully) for another 10m, where a footpath leads left, up some steps and away from the traffic.

At Watton, cross the road and find the (unsignposted) path opposite, going through a farm and across fields until you emerge back onto Broad Lane. Turn left, cross the bridge over the A35 and take an immediate right into the rest area.

West Bay meander

Distance **5.5km** Time **1 hour 30**
Terrain **clifftop paths, shingle beach,
grassy tracks, riverside path**
Map **OS Explorer 116** Access **buses from
Weymouth, Axminster and Yeovil to West
Bay; parking in West Bay (charge)**

**The sheer-faced shard of sandstone that
rears right out of the beach like an
immense orange shark fin at West Bay has
long attracted walkers and TV location
scouts. This route sends you straight up
and over iconic East Cliff, before looping
back behind the bluff at Burton and
following the serpentine coils of the River
Brit as it flows into the arms of the vibrant
harbour town where you started.**

From outside the Bridport Arms in West
Bay, stroll around the eastern wall of the
town's tidy harbour and then head left
across the fine-shingle beach. Looming
ahead is East Cliff – a stunning wall of
vertical sandstone that erupts from the
ground and changes colour like a fickle
chameleon, depending on the time of day
and the humour of the elements.

The blade-like bluff has a golden glow
when the sun is on its face, but it can
transit through a spectrum of autumnal
colours, from bright orange to earthy
brown. No matter what hue greets you,
it's always dramatic. Fitting, then, that
the cliff has starred in several TV shows,
from the title sequence of 1970s sitcom
The Fall and Rise of Reginald Perrin through to
the more recent disturbing drama
Broadchurch, starring David Tennant and
penned by *Torchwood* and *Dr Who*
scriptwriter Chris Chibnall, who lives
in nearby Bridport.

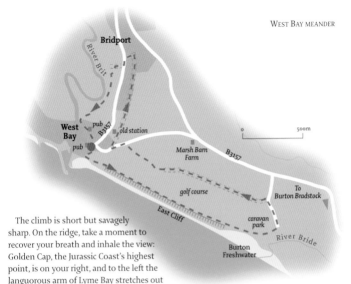

The climb is short but savagely sharp. On the ridge, take a moment to recover your breath and inhale the view: Golden Cap, the Jurassic Coast's highest point, is on your right, and to the left the languorous arm of Lyme Bay stretches out to touch Portland.

Carry on over the cliff, descending and then climbing a couple of sets of steps helpfully built into the hill, until you roll down a steep bank and reach sea level at Burton Freshwater, near the mouth of the River Bride, on a long stretch of uninterrupted coastline that ultimately joins Chesil Beach.

To explore the pretty village of Burton Bradstock, you need to cross the footbridge. This route turns left before the river, however, to wander up through the Freshwater Holiday complex, picking up the public footpath that exits the top of the park and crosses the golf course (watch out for errant balls and listen for yells of 'fore!').

Leaving the golf course, the path crosses a stile and descends to a road, where you turn left and walk towards West Bay,

watching for traffic. You can head straight back into town along this road, but a nicer option is to turn right at the car park behind the beach to explore a section of the old railway track towards Bridport.

Walk past the Sausage & Pear Station Kitchen (a restaurant on the old railway platform, where you can dine in a vintage 1911 train carriage that once transported injured British troops after the Battle of the Somme).

Follow the bridleway past the adventure playground and, after around 200m, take a left down an alleyway to the main road. Cross, turn left, then take the next right into a nameless 'Private Road'. At the end, a footpath flows left into a riverside meadow and winds along the banks of the Brit, finishing at a footbridge to the George pub in West Bay.

◀ East Cliff at West Bay

Abbotsbury and Chesil Beach

Distance **10km** Time **3 hours**
Terrain **Ridgeway and coastal footpaths,
beach and town streets** Map **OS Explorer
OL15** Access **buses from Weymouth,
Bridport and Axminster to Abbotsbury;
parking in Abbotsbury (charge)**

**Prettily positioned by the World Heritage-
listed Chesil Beach and famous for its
swannery and the 14th-century chapel of
St Catherine's that floats like a vision
above the village, Abbotsbury is a lovely
launchpad for a ramble along the South
Dorset Ridgeway, via an Iron Age castle,
returning along the coast into the
embrace of the Ilchester Arms.**

Hidden in the hilly hinterland behind the
South West Coast Path, just before Chesil
Bank's epic shingle beach reaches round to
touch the almost-isle of Portland,
Abbotsbury is a garden-rich village full of
history, and silent swans, and complete
with a fine pub. All of the above is best
appreciated after a walk through the Area of
Outstanding Natural Beauty surrounding it.

If you arrive by car, exit the town car
park, cross Rodden Row, walk directly up
Rosemary Lane, take a left on Back Street,
then look for a bridleway sign pointing
right along Blind Lane, indicating the
Hardy Monument and a hillfort.
Alternatively, from the Ilchester Arms bus
stop, walk north along Market Street, turn
right along Back Street, pass the Old
School House café and, just after the public
toilets, look for the bridleway leading left.

Follow the trail uphill, passing through
two gates. When the path forks
immediately after the second one, stay left
(the path right heads towards the Hell
Stone and Hardy Monument). When you
reach the Ridgeway, go left again, following
the obvious path along the spine of the
hill, enjoying views west along the
Jurassic Coast, and east to Portland, with
St Catherine's Chapel in the foreground.

After climbing Wears Hill and
descending to cross a quiet road, climb
again to reach Abbotsbury Castle, an Iron
Age fort with a commanding view over the

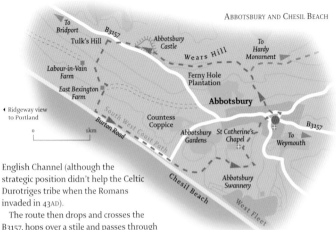

To Bridport
B3157
Tulk's Hill
Abbotsbury Castle
Wears Hill
To Hardy Monument
Labour-in-Vain Farm
East Bexington Farm
Ferny Hole Plantation
Abbotsbury
◄ Ridgeway view to Portland
South West Coast Path
Burton Road
Countess Coppice
Abbotsbury Gardens
St Catherine's Chapel
B3157
To Weymouth
0   1km
Chesil Beach
Abbotsbury Swannery
West Fleet

English Channel (although the strategic position didn't help the Celtic Durotriges tribe when the Romans invaded in 43AD).

The route then drops and crosses the B3157, hops over a stile and passes through several Bronze Age burial barrows at the National Trust-owned site at Tulk's Hill. Paths lead on to West Bexington from here, but this route descends to the coast through fields, crossing another stile to pass the pessimistically named Labour-in-Vain Farm, and then East Bexington Farm.

When you reach the beach, turn left. You can walk on the shingle, but it's better to boot along Burton Road, the laneway that shadows the shore. After about 2km, however, the road reaches a car park and elbows left to Abbotsbury's celebrated subtropical gardens, and walkers wishing to stay on the South West Coast Path (which here doubles as the Macmillan Way) are forced onto the stones.

Chesil Beach stretches all the way to Portland, creating a lagoon to the landside, with its pebbles getting larger the further east you go. While this singular shingle expanse is an extraordinary natural phenomenon, it's not the easiest terrain to traverse, and thankfully the footpath soon heads left, leading inland towards Chapel Hill. The famous swannery is on your right here. First established by Benedictine Monks, who built a monastery in Abbotsbury 1000 years ago, this is the only place on the planet where you can walk through the midst of a colony of nesting mute swans. You need to purchase a ticket to enter the swannery, however, and this walk skirts around it.

Take the first footpath branching right and walk around the base of Chapel Hill. At a bench by Chapel Coppice, a steep path leads up to St Catherine's Chapel, which is free to enter. Views east extend across Chesil Beach and Portland while west lies the great arc of Lyme Bay stretching into Devon.

Drop down into the town by the path on the other side of the hill, before cutting along an alley on the right to the rear of the Ilchester Arms. The town car park is just around the corner, by the ancient remains of St Peter's Abbey and the more modern St Nicholas' Church.

Portland circular

Distance **17km** Time **5 hours**
Terrain **footpaths, coastal tracks, clifftop
trails and streets** Map **OS Explorer OL15**
Access **buses from Dorchester and
Weymouth to Fortuneswell; parking in
Fortuneswell (charge)**

Portland, dangling precariously from the
Dorset coast by a spit of sand and a bridge,
is more rugged than the rest of this soft
county. Built tough by nature and fortified
by folk to keep prisoners in and invaders
out, even the cliffs look castellated here,
on England's Alcatraz. But this eccentric
outcrop offers beauty, art and history too.
Just don't mention rabbits...

Forming the muscular rock-veined
eastern arm of Lyme Bay, Portland's
imposing limestone cliffs stare
resolutely out to sea, taunting the
elements. The stone stands solid
here – impervious to the winds and
waves that continually scar and sculpt the
Jurassic Coast elsewhere – leaving a
fascinating promontory ripe for exploration.

Starting from central Fortuneswell,
East Street climbs bravely towards HM
Prison The Verne, before stopping dead.
A footpath continues to the elbow of
Verne Common Road, where a trail
branches right to join the Portland
Circular Path/South West Coast Path.

Go right, with the prison on your left,
into the forbidding fortifications of
The Verne, a series of historic constructions
with a grim purpose, slightly softened by
the green blanket of a nature reserve now
cast across them. Perched on Portland's
highest point, the prison occupies the site
of a defensive Victorian-era citadel, which
once bristled with guns and was protected
by a moat. Repurposed as a jail 1949-2013,
these bleak buildings now form a detention
centre for migrants.

Continue south, past Fancy's Family Farm
and a quarry, before forking left through
East Weares. At Incline Road, turn right,
then immediately left along a track, passing
a disused rifle range (left) and Young
Offenders Institute (right). After 150m, turn
left down a zigzag path to the coast.

Primitive goats gallivant between Kings
Pier and Penn's Weare, where a long-
disused railway line provides an excellent

path. Pass the remains of 15th-century Rufus Castle to Church Ope Cove, scene of Britain's first Viking Raid in 789AD.

The path briefly climbs away from the sea onto Southwell Road, skirting a quarry and landslip. It's around such quarries that rabbits received their bad reputation. The burrowers were blamed for accidents and became a symbol of misfortune, and it's still considered bad luck to mention 'rabbits' on Portland, where they're called 'underground mutton'.

After Cheyne Weares car park, the path returns to the coast to cavort around coves and sea caves to Portland Bill, Dorset's most southerly point. Winking lighthouses have warned ships away from the jagged rocks and Shambles Sandbanks here for three centuries, and beacons burned bright for millennia prior to that. An obelisk still stands as a daymark.

Wander to the viewpoint overlooking White Hole and Pulpit Rock, before skirting left of the car park to head north along the coast path, passing the upper lighthouse and walking the isle's western flank, with Lyme Bay on your left (and concrete-clad Southwell and Weston to your right). Continue past Mutton Cove and Blacknor, until the path is diverted inland by subsidence, away from West Cliff and into Tout Quarry Sculpture Park, an alfresco art space where effigies have been etched into Portland stone.

Descend into Fortuneswell via Chesil Cove, the eastern extremity of the enormous beach arcing from the mainland. Walk along Chiswell Esplanade, cross the roundabout and follow Lerret Road and Mulberry Avenue to Portland Castle, a fortification built by Henry VIII to ward off French and Spanish attacks.

Walk around the castle, tracing Liberty Road but leaning left, to a roundabout. Cross, and take the road to the right of Castletown Road, heading uphill towards 'Oceanviews'. After 25m, a footpath goes right, under a bridge and along the old Merchants Railway path. Cross East Weare Road and, at Verne Common Road, turn right and descend 100m to the corner, where a footpath leads left back to East Street.

◀ Portland west coast

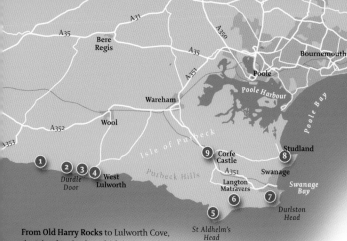

From Old Harry Rocks to Lulworth Cove, the Isle of Purbeck – which isn't an island at all – has some of the county's most iconic coastline. This is an evocative and storied shore, with curious caves that echo with smugglers' tales and wineglass-shaped bays where writers and artists go beachcombing for inspiration.

This is where the Jurassic Coast starts – or finishes, depending on which direction you're attacking the wonderful UNESCO World Heritage-listed feature from – but either way, it's an extraordinary shore to explore by foot, and it attracts adventurers of all persuasions. The endless ebb and flow of the tide has made limestone ledges for waves and walkers to dance upon, and carved arches for wild swimmers and kayakers to venture through.

Dolphins can often be seen having fun off the headlands, and the sea cliffs are alive with nesting seabirds and human climbers, squawking and talking as they cling to crags above the breaking waves. Further out, semi-submerged rock formations stare defiantly out to sea, their featured faces sculpted by the elements over aeons.

Behind all of this you will find footpaths linking follies and fossil forests frozen in time, fantastic beaches and character-soaked pubs that welcome walkers in with open arms (and, in winter, open fires) and a plethora of pumps for pouring local ales and ciders.

Like most of the South West Coast Path, the cliff-tracing trail is a rollercoaster of a ramble, with big drops and stiff climbs – from such superbly named low spots as Scratch Arse Ware and Scratchy Bottom to high points with sensational views like Bat's Head above Durdle Door.

But fabulous footpaths face inland too, including some that beat a path to the battered battlements of 1000-year-old Corfe Castle, which wears the scars of its action-packed past.

Swyre Head ▸

Isle of Purbeck

Smugglers Path to White Nothe

Distance 7km **Time** 2 hours 30
Terrain clifftop trails, footpaths,
bridleways, beach **Map** OS Explorer OL15
Access buses from Weymouth,
Dorchester, Poole and Bovington to
nearby Osmington; parking in Ringstead
National Trust car park (small charge for
non-members)

**Drift from the outskirts of the
somnambulant South Down hamlet of
Ringstead to the chalky beak of White
Nothe, where a sneaky smugglers' path
peels away to a secret beach, returning via
an eccentric little wooden church with
a heavenly vista.**

This walk wanders around the South
Down, which boasts a Bronze Age barrow
cemetery, and Ringstead – home to a
medieval ghost village, deserted in 1348
when the Black Death broke out
around Weymouth – but it's most

famous for a fictional story, inspired
by very real smugglers.

From the lower end of the elongated
National Trust car park on Falcon Barn
Lane, hop over the stile and set off along
the bridleway behind the gate, sauntering
southeast, roughly parallel to the coast.

Ignore tracks tearing off first left and
then right, and carry on past a farm. Go
straight ahead on the bridleway that
ultimately leads to Dagger's Gate, high
above Durdle Door, a supposedly haunted
spot named after the stabbing of a local
farmer in 1789 by a girl alleged to have
been a witch's daughter.

This jaunt avoids this jinxed spot,
however, taking an acute right turn at a
chalk pit by the corner of a field, just above

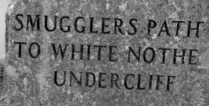

SMUGGLERS PATH
TO WHITE NOTHE
UNDERCLIFF

STEEP HAZARDOUS ROUTE

West Bottom. After about 100m you'll reach the cliff edge and a T-junction with the South West Coast Path. Bat's Head is visible off to the east, but you should turn right and walk west, where Whitenothe Cottages soon appear.

Take the track leading left, all the way to the drop-off, where a concrete WWII bunker keeps lonely watch over the curvaceous coast. From the pillbox here, a path plummets right down to the sea, taking a zigzag route down the chalky cliffs. Known as the Smugglers Path, this tumbling trail featured in J Meade Falkner's classic novel, *Moonfleet*, which tells a tale rich with shipwrecks, smugglers and swashbuckling shenanigans, all set along this stretch of the coast.

It's a steep descent and an even sterner scramble on the way back up, but it makes a good side trip for those with the energy to explore the storied shore. While you walk, listen out for birds such as wheatears and stonechats, which hang out in the impenetrable scrub that beards the undercliffs. Above, buzzards, kestrels and peregrine falcons patrol the sky.

Once back on the Coast Path, continue west, to Holworth House, before forking left to pass the tiny church of St Catherine-by-the-Sea, which looks more like a shed than a place of worship but commands a fantastic coastal view. According to some accounts, the Romantic poet John Keats spent his last night in England at Holworth (possibly penning the poem 'Bright star') before leaving for Rome, where he died of tuberculosis, aged just 25.

Just past this charismatic church, the path forks. Keep right and ascend a path, known as the Batch, up the once-famous flaming flanks of the Burning Cliff, so called because of an incident in 1826, when a rockslide sparked an oil-shale fire which smoked and smouldered for several years. All is green here now, though, and the walk wends a serpentine route beneath trees, past Marren B&B, to a T-junction with Falcon Barn Lane. Turn left to meet your starting point.

◀ Smugglers Path this way

79

Durdle dawdle

Distance **6.5km** Time **2 hours**
Terrain **clifftop trails, footpaths, beach**
Map **OS Explorer OL15** Access **limited bus
service from Wool Railway Station and
summer bus from Dorchester, Weymouth
and Swanage to Durdle Door; parking at
Durdle Door Holiday Park (charge)**

A rollercoaster ramble along the craggy
coastline that presides over the arc de
awesome that is Durdle Door, exploring
Swyre and Bat's Heads, and returning via
the Warren and Scratchy Bottom.

From the wave-washed doorstep of one
of the most recognisable natural features
in England's wild west, this cliff-hugging
escapade explores a seriously stunning
section of the South West Coast Path.

Leaving the little village of cabins,
caravans and camping spots that
comprises Durdle Door Holiday Park,
take the very obvious track down the hill
towards the beach, ignoring the turn-off
to the left which leads to the lovely
Lulworth Cove.

Quickly you reach an ice axe-shaped
headland, where information boards, stone
tablets and tourists' cameras point one
way to Durdle Door and the other to Man
o' War. Both bays boast beautiful beaches,
but if you're only going to descend into
one, wend your way down the Durdle Door
side to get a close-up view of the epic
limestone arch that has stood here with its
ankles in the sea since the Jurassic period,
some 140 million years ago.

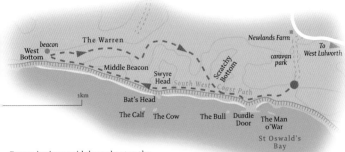

Frozen in time amid the rocks atop the arch are the petrified remains of a fossilised forest, drowned by rising tides millions of years ago and then immortalised by the Medusa effect of settling sediment.

Once you've booted around the beach for a bit, or had a wild swim in the sea, clamber back up the stairs to the headland, lean left and leave the crowds behind by walking west along a precipitous section of the South West Coast Path, which clings to the cliffs on the dramatic approach to Swyre Head.

Opposite the Bull (a rock out to sea on your left), and just before the path rears up to begin climbing the imposing hill, a small cove indents the coastline. A footpath forks right here, leading through a grassy valley known, brilliantly, as Scratchy Bottom – a moniker that came second only to Shitterton (also in Dorset) in a 2012 poll of Britain's worst place names. If the upcoming ascent looks like too much of a thigh burner, you can loop back towards the holiday village from here, cutting the walk in half.

If not, steel those quads and stride up and over Swyre Head, earning an extraordinary scoop of landscape eye-candy for your efforts. Have a gawp back at Durdle Door and Lulworth, then drop down the far side to Bat's Head, which boasts another natural arch (albeit much more modest than the big door) and good views over the Calf, Cow and Blind Cow rocks, not to mention the Portland promontory in the distance.

Keep following the South West Coast Path as it surfs along undulating white waves of rock for another 1.5km, until you spy a spiky stone beacon. Just before reaching this shard, turn right on a footpath that wends east through the Warren, hovering high above the coast path you've just walked along.

Maintain the higher ground until the path descends into the folded grass cleft of Scratchy Bottom, from the rear end of which you can retrace your footsteps to Durdle Door and the holiday village car park or bus stop.

West Lulworth loop

Distance 6.5km **Time** 3 hours
Terrain village streets, clifftop trails,
footpaths and beach **Map** OS Explorer
OL15 **Access** limited bus service from Wool
Railway Station and summer bus from
Dorchester, Weymouth and Swanage to
West Lulworth; parking opposite the
Castle Inn, West Lulworth

**Linking Lulworth Cove to Dorset's
best-known natural feature, this walk
knocks on Durdle Door before returning
via Man o' War Beach, exploring one of the
most popular parts of the entire South
West Coast Path.**

Lulworth Cove is a place of legendary
beauty, but you will have to wait until near
the end of this amble before setting eyes
on it. The wait is well spent, though,
with the walk wending via some of

the Jurassic Coast's most famous features
before arriving at the serene shores of the
celebrated cove.

Start in West Lulworth, where buses call
at the war memorial near the Castle Inn, a
thatched 16th-century pub with parking
just across the road. If this car park is full,
there's often free street parking on Church
Street, with either option preferable to the
timed car park in Lulworth Cove, which
forces you to trot against the clock. This
is a ramble that shouldn't be rushed.

Stroll west along the Main Road,
continuing towards Lulworth Cove for
about 200m beyond the junction with
Church Street, until you see a fingerpost
indicating footpaths on the opposite side
of the road. Carefully cross and follow the
footpath forking right, towards Durdle
Door, with the hump of Hambury Tout

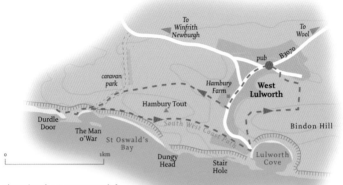

obscuring the coast on your left.

The trail eventually leans left, taking you into the busy Durdle Door car park next to the caravan park (a good place to refill water bottles). Follow the throng and descend to Durdle Door, a spectacular limestone sea arch, which has become the signature sight of the Jurassic Coast and one of Dorset's most iconic spots.

Bound down to the beach to get a close-up view, with the profile of Portland providing a picturesque backdrop, and take the plunge for a wonderful wild swimming experience if conditions allow.

Afterwards, go behind the door by hopping over the headland to explore Man o' War Beach, where ship-shaped rocks shelter a superb cove nestled within St Oswald's Bay. Tide willing, it's often possible to beach-bash right across to Dungy Head, but this walk climbs back up the steps and curls eastwards along the clifftop, via the South West Coast Path.

You can stick to the busy Coast Path here, or go off-piste and hike over the hog's back of Hambury Tout, via a trig point and the remains of a bell barrow, a burial place for a prehistoric VIP, which dates to somewhere between 1500 and 1100BC. The views from this ridge are spectacular, overlooking St Oswald's Bay and Lulworth's lovely wineglass-shaped cove.

The paths drop and conjoin just before meeting Lulworth Cove car park, which leads to the beautiful bay ringed by a horseshoe of shingle. Explore this famous shore, then rejoin the South West Coast Path by climbing steps just to the left of the ice-cream shop.

Follow this footpath through trees and up onto the brow of Bindon Hill, continuing east until you meet a crossroads at a hedgeline. Turn left along a trail tracing trees through fields, leading to School Lane. Turn left on the lane and walk into the village, pausing for a pint in the Castle Inn.

◀ Durdle Door

Lulworth Cove to Fossil Forest

Distance **4.5km** Time **2 hours**
Terrain **clifftop trails, footpaths, beach, nature reserves and town streets**
Map **OS Explorer OL15** Access **limited bus service from Wool Railway Station and summer bus from Dorchester, Weymouth and Swanage to Lulworth Cove; parking at Lulworth Cove (charge)**

This loop of lovely Lulworth Cove takes cliff combers to a surprisingly seldom-visited headland, with sensational views to Durdle Door, and the fringe of a petrified forest.

From Lulworth Visitor Centre, go past the Museum of Jurassic Marine Life and walk west, through the car park, along the South West Coast Path towards Durdle Door. Just beyond the parking area, however, fork left, leaving the Coast Path to follow a trail through fields.

The path potters through trees before meeting a T-junction. Turn right and follow this to Dungy Head, which offers eye-popping views across St Oswald's Bay, Man o' War Rock and Durdle Door. It's possible (rockfalls willing) to descend to sea level here, via a steep path, and even – at low tide – to beach-bash right around to Man o' War Beach and Durdle Door, but there's a safer way to explore these places.

Instead, take the trail leading left before the path begins to descend, and trace this as it tiptoes around the clifftops, before elbowing left through trees to join Britwell Drive. (Note: this short section does run very close to the precipitous cliffs and isn't recommended for walkers with children or dogs off lead, who are best advised to return directly to Britwell Drive by turning 180 degrees and walking straight after enjoying the Dungy Head vista, instead of taking the left turn.)

Stay on Britwell Drive until the South West Coast Path forks right, leading to Stair

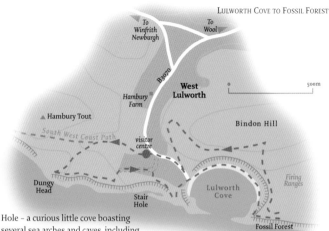

Hole – a curious little cove boasting several sea arches and caves, including Cathedral Cavern, plus an interesting geological feature known as the Lulworth crumple, where lines in the limestone walls appear to fold and flutter like rock ribbons.

Wander around the western arm of Lulworth Cove, enjoying the view across this impossibly pretty puddle, before briefly rejoining the Coast Path to reach the beach by the Boat Shed Café.

Unless the tide is really high (in which case, grab a coffee while it turns, or reverse the following section) you can walk across the beautiful beach to steps climbing cliffs at the far end. Ascend these into trees and explore the eastern arm of the bay. Eventually, however, you run into a big fence, which announces the beginning of a firing range.

The Ministry of Defence (MOD) have long commandeered a huge swathe of countryside east of Lulworth and access is restricted to times when live firing isn't taking place. On the other side of this fence lies an ancient fossilised forest of cycad trees that were alive in the Jurassic period (144 million years ago), until sea levels rose and submerged them for millennia.

Although access is currently further frustrated by a recent rockfall, this petrified forest and other features – including Smugglers Cave, Mupe Rocks and Worbarrow Bay – can be visited by foot when the 'Range Walks' are open (most weekends).

This open-all-hours route, however, turns around to climb high above Lulworth Cove, via a steep footpath with 336 steps that shadows the MOD fence as it ascends Bindon Hill, a prime habitat for butterflies in summer. At the top, the South West Coast Path lurches left, tracing the treeline before turning left again and dropping back to the western corner of the cove. Turn right and walk up the road to the visitor centre.

St Aldhelm's Head

Distance 8km Time 3 hours
Terrain footpaths, coastal trails,
country lanes and village streets
Map OS Explorer OL15 Access buses
from Swanage to Worth Matravers;
parking (charge)

Secret coves, curious caves, sculpted
stone, wind-whipped waves, wonderful
wildlife and an evocative headland define
this walk, which starts and finishes
outside a pub with all the requisite
gravitational pulling power to get you up
the gradients once you're within wishing
distance of its doors.

From Worth Matravers car park, put your
beer blinkers on to stroll past the Square &
Compass pub into the village, and bear left
at the duck pond, along Pikes Lane. Go
past the turning for Seacombe and take the
second left, following the lane to a
footpath which leads through fields and
along a stream to Winspit, a disused quarry
on the coast.

Purbeck quarries date back more than
300 years, but the caves that honeycomb

the cliffs here are now home to a colony of
greater horseshoe bats – one of Britain's
biggest species. Some of the caverns and
tunnels appear to be held up entirely by
pretty precarious pillars of stone and the
whole spot has a slightly surreal feel,
which is why it's been used to shoot
scenes for *Doctor Who* – playing the planet
Skaro in one episode of 'Destiny of the
Daleks' – among other sci-fi shows,
including *Blake 7*.

The craggy terrain here is better suited
to nimble climbers than tin-can monsters,
but big red signs make it abundantly clear
that the private owners do not encourage
cliff clambering or caving, and that any
exploring you might do is entirely at your
own risk.

Continue west along the South West
Coast Path towards St Aldhelm's Head,
passing several extraordinary wind-etched
monoliths and rock formations, which
lend the headland an ambience that is

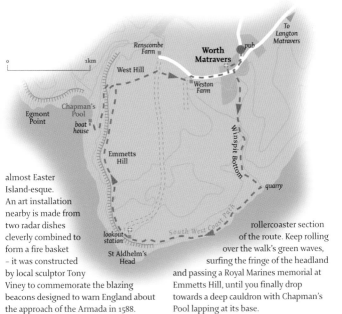

almost Easter Island-esque. An art installation nearby is made from two radar dishes cleverly combined to form a fire basket – it was constructed by local sculptor Tony Viney to commemorate the blazing beacons designed to warn England about the approach of the Armada in 1588.

Carry on, past St Aldhelm's Chapel, with a history dating back over 800 years (although the current chapel was built in the 19th century), a mighty stone throne with a majestic view, and the National Coastwatch Institution (NCI) Lookout Station, which observes the eternally galloping white horses of St Alban's Race. You can pop your head into the Lookout Station (for which the NCI pays a lease to the landowner of 'one crab per annum') unless an emergency is unfolding.

A century of super steep steps then sends the path plunging down before rearing back up almost as savagely, beginning a rollercoaster section of the route. Keep rolling over the walk's green waves, surfing the fringe of the headland and passing a Royal Marines memorial at Emmetts Hill, until you finally drop towards a deep cauldron with Chapman's Pool lapping at its base.

To explore this cove closely, leave the South West Coast Path and descend a dramatic spur trail (some sections complete with ropes to aid scramblers) to the Boat House, which was a Lifeboat Station for a short period.

Retrace your steps to West Hill, then head back to Worth Matravers through the car park near Renscombe (a pioneering centre of radar research and development after WWII) and Weston Farm. A laneway passes the village hall and St Nicholas of Myra, one of Dorset's oldest churches, leading to the altar of ale and crisps at the Square & Compass.

◀ St Aldhelm's Head monolith

Dancing Ledge

Distance **7km** Time **2 hours 30**
Terrain **footpaths, coastal trails,
country lanes and village streets**
Map **OS Explorer OL15**
Access **bus from Swanage to Worth
Matravers; parking (charge)**

**Shuffle on down to nature's dancefloor
from one of Dorset's most iconic pubs,
bust a few moves as the waves rock a
rhythm on the limestone ledge, and then
scoot back for a beer via a cheeky Scratch
Arse Ware shortcut to the Priest's Way.**

The only problem about starting beside
the Square & Compass in Worth Matravers
is that it's the kind of walker-friendly
wonderpub that can tempt you out of ever
taking off on a trek in the first place. Steel
yourself, though, because a post-pootle
pint tastes ten times better.

From the car park, walk down the hill,
with the pub on your left (stay strong).
At the T-junction, bear right and continue
down the road. Just before you reach the
village pond, take a left down Pike Lane,
and then another immediate left,
following a footpath fingersign pointing
towards Seacombe.

The lane passes houses, then segues to a
footpath, which hops across fields,
meeting another track after about 750m.
Turn right along this path and descend
through Seacombe Bottom to a disused
quarry right on the rocky shore.

Looking out across the English Channel,
Seacombe Cliffs rear off to your left, the
indented coastline looking like a lonely
jigsaw puzzle piece awaiting its match.
Walk along the undulating clifftop path,
chugging along above secret sea caves
where sneaky smugglers once stashed
their swag.

Before you reach Dancing Ledge proper,
Hedbury Quarry presents an intriguing
pitstop. The little raised cove comes
complete with an old cannon and almost
constantly contains climbers, carabiners
clanking as they clamber up the cliffs.

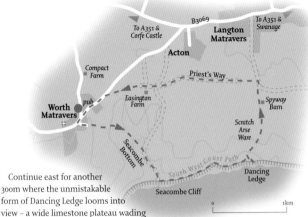

Continue east for another 300m where the unmistakable form of Dancing Ledge looms into view – a wide limestone plateau wading recklessly into the waves. During certain tides, the restless rippling of the sea makes the rock look as though it's doing a jig – a phenomena that bequeathed this fantastic feature its name.

There are more caves at the back of this cove – which were once quarried for stone – but they're blocked off. Dancing Ledge is another sport climbing hotspot, and there will be people clinging to the crags most times of the day.

Getting down onto the rock shelf itself entails a small scramble, but it's worth it. A small bathing pool has been blasted into the limestone here, with the water warmed by the sun between tides. This is the place for a plunge, as swimming in the open sea is unsafe – there are no easy exit points, and people have been pulled beneath the plateau by currents.

After climbing back out of the cove, you'll see two paths heading north, up the hill (as opposed to continuing along the South West Coast Path). Take the right-hand option, going past Scratch Arse Ware on your left ('ware' being a local term for rough land used for grazing), to walk via the National Trust-owned Spyway Barn. This place, which owes its name to smuggling shenanigans, has a display room offering details about local wildlife and history.

At the top of the hill you'll meet a junction with a well-established path, the Priest's Way, an ancient trail named after a medieval priest who walked between Swanage and Worth Matravers attending to his flock.

Turn left and follow in the sandal steps of the priest, through Easington Farm. Stay left at the junction just past the farm, and keep left again when you meet the road. Enter Worth Matravers village and wander down to the Square & Compass for that long-awaited and well-deserved ale.

Durlston Head Globe trotter

Distance 7km Time 2 hours
Terrain footpaths, coastal trails, nature
reserves and town streets
Map OS Explorer OL15 Access buses from
Bournemouth, Dorchester, Poole,
Wareham and Weymouth to Swanage;
parking at Broad Road, Swanage (charge)

Stroll around the Great Globe from the
seductive seaside town of Swanage,
starting near the pier and going point-to-
point from Peveril to Anvil via Durlston
Castle and Tilly Whim Caves, returning
through two nature reserves.

Set off from Prince Albert Gardens, with
the swoop of Swanage Bay to your left, and
stroll along the South West Coast Path,
past the pier and sailing club, towards
Peveril Point.

Just before the RNLI Lifeboat Station
you'll pass Wellington Clock Tower, which
stood at the southern entrance to London
Bridge for a decade in the mid-19th

century, until it started obstructing the Big
Smoke's traffic and was relocated here.

The wicked waters off Peveril Point have
claimed numerous ships over the years,
including an entire Viking fleet on its way
from Wareham to Exeter in 877AD, an
accident often hailed as a victory for Alfred
the Great (Swanage's Alfred Monument
celebrates this myth).

The Lookout Station keeps an eye on
modern shipping, while walkers gaze across
the bay to Old Harry Rocks and the Isle of
Wight beyond. Turn your back on this vista,
walk around the point and embrace a new
view, this one of Durlston Bay and
headland, which you are about to explore.

The Coast Path skirts the cliffs for a short
while, before meeting the streets of south
Swanage at Belle Vue Road. Go left, past
several flats, keeping your eyes peeled for a

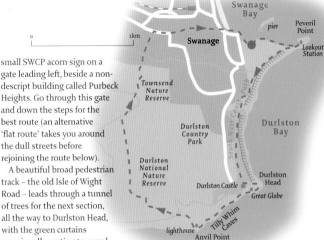

small SWCP acorn sign on a gate leading left, beside a nondescript building called Purbeck Heights. Go through this gate and down the steps for the best route (an alternative 'flat route' takes you around the dull streets before rejoining the route below).

A beautiful broad pedestrian track – the old Isle of Wight Road – leads through a tunnel of trees for the next section, all the way to Durlston Head, with the green curtains occasionally parting to reveal great coastal views.

At the junction, turn left and walk around the sea side of Durlston Castle, a Victorian folly built by local businessman George Burt in 1886-87, essentially as a restaurant for guests at his country park. Quotes from various authors, including a particularly pertinent stanza from Alfred Lord Tennyson's 'The Palace of Art', are engraved in rocks around the building.

Perhaps the Jurassic Coast's most impressive man-made feature is found just around the head, in the spherical shape of the Great Globe, a 40-ton scale representation of our planet as it was in 1889, sculpted from Portland stone.

Look out for dolphins around Durlston; pods of the playful mammals are often spotted here, and the head is also home to hundreds of species of seabirds.

Continue to Tilly Whim Caves, historic quarries where Purbeck stone was once mined and smugglers' contraband stashed. Rockfalls have made it unsafe to explore the tunnels, now haunted by hordes of bats, but the entrances are still very visible.

At Anvil Point Lighthouse, turn right, head inland and navigate northwest, then north along paths dissecting Durlston National Nature Reserve (follow the pink butterfly signs of the 'Wildlife Trail') into Townsend Nature Reserve, where old quarry entrances burrow into the ground.

Just past one such hole, the trail exits the reserve and enters Hoburne Park housing estate. Alleyways lead to Cowlease and Swanage High Street, where you turn right and return to the seafront.

◀ The Great Globe

Studland and Old Harry Rocks

Distance 8km **Time** 3 hours
Terrain coastal, cliff and ridgeline
footpaths, some quiet roads and laneways
Map OS Explorer OL15 **Access** bus from
Poole and Swanage; National Trust car
park, Middle Beach, Studland (charge for
non-members)

**From war-scarred Studland Bay to the
iconic chalk stacks of Handfast Point,
returning along the ridgeline route
across beautiful Ballard Down, this
foreland foray offers amblers some of
the South Coast's very best views.**

Thanks to its position, facing France,
strategic Studland Bay has historically
been a place where preparations are made
to both repel and launch attacks, and the
savage scratch marks of war still feature
large in the topography here.

It's barely a 50m meander from the
bottom exit of the car park to
the sandy seafront, but just
behind the beach huts a grey set of
'Dragon's Teeth' still snarl – rows of
pointed concrete blocks, punctuated by
ditches that once bristled with mines,
forming anti-tank defences during a period
of the Second World War when a Nazi
invasion looked frighteningly likely.

Turn right along the shore, before bending
briefly inland at the café. After about 60m,
turn left on the South West Coast Path to
find Fort Henry, an observation bunker where
Churchill, Eisenhower, King George VI, Field
Marshal Montgomery and Acting Admiral
Mountbatten once watched Allied forces
assemble on the beach below to rehearse the
biggest live-ammunition drill of WWII. Enter
and peer through the slit window in the thick
wall for a view far more serene than the scene
would have seemed on 18 April 1944, six
weeks before D-Day.